MW01532481

BLOND'S ESSAY SERIES

TORTS ESSAY QUESTIONS

S&G SULZBURGER & GRAHAM PUBLISHING Ltd.
PO Box 20058 • New York, NY 10025

BLOND'S® ESSAY SERIES

TORTS ESSAY QUESTIONS

by
Daniel J. DeSario
William Carstanjen
Robert Connors
Susan R. Friedman

edited by
Brett Harris

Copyright 1992 © Sulzburger & Graham Publishing, Ltd.
All rights reserved — No part of this book may be reproduced by any electronic or other means without written permission from the publisher.

ISBN 0-945819-21-8

Printed in The United States of America

INTRODUCTION

Blond's Essay Questions are designed to help you focus on the most important component of your law school class: the final examination. Writing successful law school examination answers requires fundamentally different skills than those required for class preparation. By the end of the semester professors are no longer interested in your knowledge of particular cases. True mastery of the law is best displayed, they feel, by your ability to find legal issues in any given factual situation. Most often the highest grade goes to the student who spots the most issues.

For many students, this type of examination is unlike any they have experienced in their undergraduate studies. For one thing, quantity is often more important than quality: it is better to spot thirty issues and leave them unresolved than to fully develop a single claim from pleadings to appeal. Furthermore, organization of the essay is more important than ever before. Given the complicated factual situations provided, it is all too easy to get lost in your thought process, leaving your analysis a tangled mess of doctrine and case law.

Blond's Essay Questions show you how to organize and write top-grade law school examination answers. Twenty-five challenging questions are provided, along with a step-by-step method for answering each. The Issue/Fact Ladder builds a framework, linking each issue to the relevant facts that support it. The Outline of Issues gives each answer a logical structure and form. Finally, the Substantive Answer ties the two together, providing an organized and concise response to the questions posed. You will notice that the Substantive Answers differ in style and degree of polish; this was done to demonstrate that different approaches may be equally successful. It is important to remember that your writing style may differ from our authors'; the methodology, rather than the ability to recite our finished product verbatim, is what you should learn from this book.

QUESTION 1

Jill, a married public school teacher, became involved several years ago in an affair with Jack, her principal at Hudson High School. Jill broke off the relationship after consulting with her minister. Since that time, Jack has attempted to continue the affair. He called Jill at her home, threatened to make a full disclosure to Jill's husband, and, without cause, charged her with violations of school regulations.

Because of Jack's harassment, Jill resigned her position at Hudson effective at the end of the school year, and applied for a new teaching position for the next school year at Clark High School in an adjoining school district. She was notified by Clark officials that her application had been accepted. A few days later, however, she received notice from Clark that upon reconsideration her application had been "finally rejected."

Jill was advised by a Clark official that, in response to Clark's inquiry, Jack had reported that Jill was a woman of poor moral character who often appeared at work with alcohol on her breath. The Clark official stated that her application had been rejected based on the information supplied by Jack. In fact, Jill had never appeared at work with alcohol on her breath.

Jill commenced an action against Jack seeking damages. She alleged that she is unable to find employment with other schools because schools routinely make inquires to former school employers; that she is unable to find other employment, except as a waitress for two-thirds the compensation she could earn as a teacher; that she has declined such other employment; and that because of fear and emotional trauma, she has suffered and is continuing to suffer irreparable injury.

What are Jill's rights, if any, against Jack? Discuss.

ISSUE/FACT LADDER

Issue	Facts
Paragraph 1 Invasion of Privacy	Jack called Jill at home and threatened to make full disclosure to Jill's husband.
Paragraph 1 Malice	Without cause, Jack charged her with violations of school regulations.
Paragraph 2 Interference With an Existing Contract	Because of Jack's harassment, Jill resigned her position at Hudson.
Paragraph 2 Interference With a Prospective Advantage	Jill was rejected for a position at Clark High School after Jack made false statements about her character.
Paragraph 3 Defamation	Jack had reported that Jill was a woman of poor moral character who often appeared at work with alcohol on her breath.
Paragraph 3 Malice	In fact, Jill has never appeared at work with alcohol on her breath.
Paragraph 3 Privilege	The information which was the basis for Clark rejecting Jill's application was provided by Jack, Jill's former employer.
Paragraph 4 Damages	Jill was unable to find employment with other schools. She alleged that she suffered emotional trauma and has sustained irreparable injury.
Paragraph 4 Duty to Mitigate Damages	Jill was able to gain employment as a waitress for two-thirds the compensation she could earn as a teacher, but declined such employment.

OUTLINE OF ISSUES

What are Jill's rights, if any, against Jack? Discuss.

I. Invasion of Privacy

    A. Intrusion Upon Seclusion

    B. False Light

II. Tortious Interference with Advantageous Relationships

    A. Interference with an Existing Contract

    B. Interference with a Prospective Advantage

    C. Duty to Mitigate Damages

III.   Defamation

    A. Defamatory Statement

    B. Publication

    C. Fault

    D. Damages

IV.   Intentional Infliction of Emotional Distress

SUBSTANTIVE ANSWER

I. Invasion of Privacy: Jill could bring an action for invasion of privacy against Jack under the theories of intrusion upon seclusion and false light.

A. Intrusion Upon Seclusion: Jill has a right to be free from intrusion upon the solitude and seclusion of her private life and affairs. Jack's action of calling her at home would not fulfill the requirement that the intrusion be highly offensive to a reasonable person. Unless Jack's calls were persistent, it is unlikely that she would recover under this theory.

B. False Light: Jill has a right to be free from publicity which places her in a false light. While Jack's statements to Clark about her drinking portrayed her in a false light, they were only made to the officials at Clark High School. It is doubtful that this would satisfy the requirement that the person be placed before the public eye in a false light.

II. Tortious Interference with Advantageous Relationships: Jill could also bring an action for tortious interference with advantageous relationships under the theories of interference with an existing contract and interference with a prospective advantage.

A. Interference with an Existing Contract: The facts state that Jill resigned from school because of Jack's harassment. She could not recover for the tort of interference with an existing contract because that only applies when a third party induces another party to breach a contract with a plaintiff (e.g., if the school fired Jill based on Jack's actions). She may, however, recover under the closely related tort of interference with a plaintiff's own performance of a contract because Jack's harassment made it burdensome for Jill to complete her contract.

B. Interference with a Prospective Advantage: Jack will also be liable for interfering with Jill's prospective teaching contract with Clark High School. She was informed that her application was rejected, after an initial acceptance, because of the information supplied by Jack. Jack would be unable to invoke any of the privileges to this tort because he acted out of malice when he supplied the false information to the Clark officials.

C. Duty to Mitigate Damages: A plaintiff cannot recover damages for injuries which a reasonably prudent person would have avoided. Jack may argue that Jill breached her duty to mitigate damages when she declined employment as a waitress because the job was for two-thirds the compensation she could earn as a teacher. However, most courts have not extended the duty to mitigate damages this far. Plaintiffs who seek lost income damages have no duty to obtain work outside their chosen profession.

III.   Defamation: To bring an action for defamation Jill must prove that Jack intentionally or negligently published a defamatory statement, causing damages to Jill.

A. Defamatory Statement: Jack's statement that Jill was a woman of poor moral character who often appeared at work with alcohol on her breath is defamatory because it caused injury to Jill's reputation as a teacher. Jack will probably assert that he had a qualified privilege to make reports following inquiries by Clark because he was Jill's former employer. However, by making statements that he knew to be false, Jack acted with malice and is barred from invoking this privilege.

B. Publication: Publication occurs when a defamatory statement is conveyed and understood by a third person. Jack conveyed his defamatory statements to Clark officials who obviously understood them since the statements influenced their decision to reject Jill's application for employment.

C. Fault: A defendant is at fault for a defamatory statement if it was intentionally or negligently published. Jack deliberately told Clark officials about the defamatory statements in question.

D. Damages: If Jack's report was written, it would be libel and the court will presume damages. If his report was oral, she would normally have to prove special damages. However, since the report involved an attack on Jill's business reputation, it is considered slander per se and damages would be presumed. Jill may also be able to recover for punitive damages since Jack's defamatory statements were made with malice.

IV.   Intentional Infliction of Emotional Distress: Finally, Jill will also bring an action against Jack for intentional infliction of emotional distress. It appears that Jack's conduct satisfies the requirement that the conduct which caused the emotional distress be extreme and outrageous. He deliberately told lies about Jill's moral character. However, it would be difficult to recover under this theory unless the irreparable injuries which accompanied her distress were physical injuries. Accompanying physical injuries are often necessary to prove that the distress was severe.

QUESTION 2

Fred purchased a new house in a winter resort area from Bildco, the builder/developer of the resort. Heavy snowfalls were not unusual for the area. During the first winter following completion of the house, a portion of the roof collapsed from the weight of a heavy snowfall. Pete, a friend of Fred, was using the house for the weekend and was injured.

The plans and specifications which had been used in building the house had previously been prepared by Art, an independent architect for one of Bildco's developments in the southern part of the state where it never snowed. Art was not consulted prior to use of the plans and specifications in the winter resort area, as Bildco was free to use the plans anywhere. Art knew that Bildco had developments all over the state.

1. What are Pete's rights, if any, against Art? Discuss.

2. What are Pete's rights, if any, against Bildco? Discuss.

3. What are Pete's rights, if any, against Fred? Discuss.

ISSUE/FACT LADDER

Issue	Facts
Paragraph 1 Foreseeability	Heavy snowfalls were not unusual for the area.
Paragraph 1 Damages	A portion of the roof collapsed, injuring Pete.
Paragraph 1 Causation	The roof collapsed from the weight of the snow.
Paragraph 1 Licensee	Pete, a friend of Fred, was using the house for the weekend.
Paragraph 2 Privity	The plans for the house had been prepared by Art, an independent architect.
Paragraph 2 Use of Product for an Unintended Purpose	The plans had been prepared for a house in one of Bildco's developments in the southern part of the state where it never snowed. However, Bildco had been free to use the plans anywhere.
Paragraph 2 Foreseeability	Art was not consulted prior to the use of the plans, but knew that Bildco had developments all over the state.

OUTLINE OF ISSUES

1. What are Pete's rights, if any, against Art? Discuss.
2. What are Pete's rights, if any, against Bildco? Discuss.
3. What are Pete's rights, if any, against Fred? Discuss.

I. Pete v. Art

    A. Negligence

        1. Duty

        2. Breach

        3. Causation

        4. Damages

    B. Products Liability

II. Pete v. Bildco

    Products Liability

    A. Negligence

        1. Duty and Breach

        2. Causation and Damages

    B. Implied Warranty

    C. Strict Products Liability

III. Pete v. Fred

    Negligence of Landowner to Licensee

SUBSTANTIVE ANSWER

I. Pete v. Art

Pete could bring an action against Art under the theories of negligence and products liability, but probably would not prevail under either theory due to causation problems.

A. Negligence: To prevail in a suit under the theory of negligence Pete must show that Art owed him a duty of care and that Art breached that duty, causing him damages.

1. Duty: Art had a duty to act as a reasonably prudent person would to avoid causing an unreasonable risk of harm to another.

2. Breach: Although Art was not consulted, he knew that Bildco had developments statewide, and should have informed Bildco that the plans were not suitable for snowy areas.

3. Causation: The causal link between Art's defective plans and Pete's injuries is quite tenuous. Bildco's negligent use of the plans in a snowy area without consulting Art or another architect, when the plans were originally drawn for a warm area, may be a superseding intervening cause.

4. Damages: If it is proven that Art is liable, Pete must plead and prove actual damages in order to recover. He may receive compensatory damages for the injuries he suffered when the roof collapsed.

B. Products Liability: An action against Art under a products liability theory will probably fail since the production of plans and specifications may be regarded as a service, as opposed to a product. In the event that it is regarded as a product, it would still be difficult to recover since the intervening acts of Bildco pose the same problem of causation as mentioned earlier.

II. Pete v. Bildco

Pete could probably bring a successful products liability action against Bildco.

Products Liability: The products liability action may be brought under the theories of negligence, implied warranty of merchantability, and strict products liability.

A. Negligence: Pete should be able to recover in a products liability action based on Bildco's negligence.

1. Duty and Breach: Bildco had a duty to ensure that the buildings it sold were designed in a reasonably safe way. Pete could likely prove that reliance on Art's plans without consulting Art or another architect was unreasonable, since the plans had originally been drawn for a warm-area development. The ultimate responsibility for the poor design of the home falls on the builder since its duty is probably nondelegable.

2. Causation and Damages: "But for" Bildco's unreasonable use of Art's plans, the roof would not have been constructed with the defect which caused Pete's injuries. The heavy snowfall is not a superseding cause because snowfall was common and, thus, foreseeable. Because Bildco's breach was the proximate cause of Pete's injuries, Pete should be able to recover in a products liability action based on Bildco's negligence.

B. Implied Warranty: An implied warranty of merchantability implies minimum standards of quality and safety. Pete might recover for a breach of this implied warranty if he sues in one of the minority jurisdictions which recognizes an implied warranty of merchantability for sales of real property. Although Pete was not the homeowner, most states extend the protection of an implied warranty to a buyer's family and guests. This is called horizontal privity.

C. Strict Products Liability: Pete may recover in a strict products liability action based on design defects. The roof was unreasonably dangerous since it was designed in such a way that it could not withstand the weight of the snow. Pete may recover compensatory damages for his injuries since they were proximately caused by the design defect. Again, the snow was not a superseding cause because it was foreseeable.

III.   Pete v. Fred

Negligence: Pete would not be entitled to recover from Fred under the theory of negligence. Pete had a privilege to enter and remain on Fred's land, and is considered a licensee. Because Pete was a licensee, Fred, as the landowner, only had a duty to warn him of conditions on the land which Fred knew to pose an unreasonable risk of harm. Further, Fred had no duty to inspect for potentially dangerous conditions that might injure Pete. Fred did not breach his duty to Pete because he was unaware of the roof's weakness. Because Fred did not breach his duty to Pete, Pete cannot recover from Fred under a negligence theory.

QUESTION 3

Mag, Inc. publishes a magazine and operates a laboratory for advertisers' merchandise. Mag authorizes the use of a symbol that says "Mag Seal of Approval" when Mag's test indicate that the product is safe and wholesome.

Mag examined samples of Tint hair coloring by Tintco, Inc. Mag's tests indicated that Tint was effective and satisfactory. Mag authorized Tintco to use its seal of approval in advertising Tint and on the product itself. Neither Tintco nor Mag was aware that when Tint is brought into direct contact with Balm, an infrequently used scalp medicine, Tint causes hair to turn purple.

Samantha, a contestant in a beauty contest, used Tint on her hair while it was still wet with Balm. As a result, Samantha's hair turned purple and she had to withdraw from the contest. She had been regarded as the favorite. To Samantha's embarrassment her hair discoloration persisted until her hair grew out.

1. What are Samantha's rights against Tintco? Discuss.

2. What are Samantha's rights against Mag? Discuss.

ISSUE/FACT LADDER

Issue	Facts
Paragraph 1 Express Warranty	Mag authorizes the use of a symbol that says "Mag Seal of Approval" when Mag's tests indicate that the product is safe and wholesome.
Paragraph 2 Negligence	Mag examined samples of Tintco's hair coloring product. Mag's tests indicated that Tint was effective and satisfactory.
Paragraph 2 Express Warranty	Mag authorized Tintco to use its seal of approval in advertising Tint and on the product itself.
Paragraph 3 Product Used For Its Intended Purpose	Samantha, a contestant in a beauty contest, used Tint on her hair, as was intended by Tintco.
Paragraph 3 Damages	Samantha's hair turned purple and she had to withdraw from the contest. She had been regarded as the favorite.
Paragraph 3 Negligent Infliction of Emotional Distress	To Samantha's embarrassment, her hair discoloration persisted until her hair grew out.

OUTLINE OF ISSUES

1. What are Samantha's rights against Tintco? Discuss.
2. What are Samantha's rights against Mag? Discuss.

I. Samantha v. Tintco

   Products Liability Theories

   A. Negligence

      1. Duty

      2. Breach

      3. Causation

      4. Damages

   B. Warranty

      1. Implied Warranty

         a. Fitness for a Particular Purpose

         b. Merchantability

      2. Express Warranty

   C. Strict Products Liability

      1. Defective Design

      2. Failure to Warn

II. Samantha v. Mag

   A. Negligent Misrepresentation

   B. Express Warranty

SUBSTANTIVE ANSWER

I. Samantha v. Tintco

Samantha should bring an action against Tintco under a products liability theory.

A. Negligence: For an action to be brought under negligence, Samantha must prove duty, breach of duty, causation and damages.

1. Duty: Tintco owed Samantha a duty to make a safe product.

2. Breach: Tintco breached its duty when it failed to properly test Tint and Balm together and failed to warn foreseeable users of the possible dangers from its product.

3. Causation: Samantha was an actual user of Tint. Though the hair discoloration was caused by both Balm and Tint, the use of Tint may be regarded as the proximate cause since Tintco breached its duty of care. The fact that the use of Balm may be a proximate cause as well would not relieve Tintco of liability.

4. Damages: Samantha should be able to recover damages for her embarrassment and blemished reputation as a result of her hair turning purple.

B. Warranty: Samantha might be able to recover for Tintco's breach of its implied or express warranty.

1. Implied Warranty: Tintco was a regular seller of this product and by offering this product for sale it created an implied warranty of merchantability that the product was suitable for its intended use. Samantha may recover since the product was not fit to be used as a hair coloring agent as is evidenced by the discoloring of her hair.

2. Express Warranty: Samantha could argue that by using Mag's Seal of Approval on its advertisements and products, Tintco created an express warranty that the product was safe and wholesome. A seller must describe a product in a certain way to create an express warranty. Samantha may argue that Tintco guaranteed the product's quality by using a well-known symbol on its product that was associated with quality.

C. Strict Products Liability: Tintco was the manufacturer of Tint, and Samantha was a foreseeable user of that product. Tintco may be strictly liable if Samantha can prove that Tint's design was defective or that Tintco failed to warn her of a danger that they should have known of.

1. Defective Design: Samantha could also argue that Tint was defectively designed because it was not as safe as a reasonable consumer would expect it to be when used

for its intended purpose. She would also have to prove that the design defect caused the injury she sustained and that there was a practical and safer alternative design (this should not be too difficult).

2. Failure to Warn: Since Tintco did not know about Tint's adverse affects when combined with Balm, Tintco will be liable if Samantha can prove that a reasonable person in Tintco's position would have known of the dangers. Although the chance that one might use both products is remote, it should be foreseeable to a manufacturer of hair coloring products that both products might be used at the same time. Therefore, Tintco should have known of the possibility of hair discoloration when its product was used with Balm and warned its consumers adequately.

II. Samantha v. Mag

A. Negligent Misrepresentation: Although Mag may have honestly believed Tintco's product was safe, it may be liable for negligent misrepresentation because it failed to exercise reasonable care in determining whether the product was actually safe. Samantha will recover for her injuries if she can prove she was justified in relying on Mag's endorsement. Since Mag was known for its products safety testing and was assumed to have superior knowledge compared with the average consumer, it was reasonable for Samantha to rely on their endorsement of Tintco's product.

B. Express Warranty: Mag may be considered a seller of Tint along with Tintco because its "Seal of Approval" is probably the reason many people bought Tint. If so, the same considerations used to determine whether Tintco created an express warranty will be used to determine whether Mag created an express warranty.

QUESTION 4

Upon retirement, Bill and Jane Mason purchased a specially designed, custom-built mobile home trailer from a dealer for $65,000. They made a down payment of $10,000 and the dealer retained a security interest for the balance of the purchase price. The Masons moved with the mobile home into a space rented from Dream Park, where they paid monthly rent.

Several months later, the trailer was removed from Dream Park by agents of The Finance Company. Bill protested the removal and suffered a broken leg when he refused to step down and fell from the step of the trailer as it was being pulled away. He has since been hospitalized.

Because of mental distress suffered when she learned of these events, Jane has been hospitalized and is under the care of a physician.

The trailer is now in the possession of The Finance Company and is being advertised for sale.

The Finance Company had erroneously repossessed the Mason's trailer, believing it was the property of another party who had defaulted on a debt that was secured by a mortgage on a trailer similar to the Mason's.

The fair rental value of the Mason's trailer is $1,000 a month. A small section of the trailer was dented while it was in Finance's possession. It would cost $500 to repair the dent, but the damage is neither serious nor noticeable. The Mason's clothes and other personal possessions are missing from the trailer. The Masons replaced such personal property at a cost of $5,000.

What are the rights of Bill and Jane, and what relief is available to them? Discuss.

ISSUE/FACT LADDER

Issue	Facts
Paragraph 1 Damages	The trailer had a value of $65,000. Bill and Jane paid a $10,000 down payment.
Paragraph 2 Vicarious Liability	The trailer was removed from Dream Park by agents of The Finance Company.
Paragraph 2 Assault and Battery	The Finance Company removed the trailer from under Bill as he protested the removal, causing him to hit the ground and suffer a broken leg.
Paragraph 3 Negligent Infliction of Emotional Distress	Jane suffered severe emotional distress when she learned of the events.
Paragraph 4 Trespass to Chattel / Conversion	The trailer is in the possession of The Finance Company who is advertising it for sale.
Paragraph 5 Mistake as to Possession of the Trailer	The Finance Company acted under a mistaken belief as to the owner of the trailer.
Paragraph 6 Damages	The cost to repair a dent in the trailer was $500. The cost to replace the personal property from the trailer was $5000. The fair rental value of the trailer is $1000 per month.

OUTLINE OF ISSUES

What are the rights of Bill and Jane, and what relief is available to them?

I. Battery

    A. Harmful or Offensive Contact

    B. Intent to Make Contact

II. Assault

    A. Awareness

    B. Intent

III.   Damages for Battery and Assault

IV.   Infliction of Emotional Distress

    A. Intentional

    B. Negligent

V. Trespass to Chattel

VI.   Conversion

SUBSTANTIVE ANSWER

I. Battery: Bill has a right to be free from harmful or offensive contact. This right is protected under the tort of battery.

A. Harmful or Offensive Contact: The agents of The Finance Company caused Bill to make a harmful contact with the ground when they pulled the trailer away while he stood on its steps. The fact that the agents did not themselves touch Bill is irrelevant, since the harmful or offensive contact of a battery may be inflicted either directly or indirectly.

B. Intent: In order to have committed a battery, the agents must have either intended that Bill make contact with the ground, or have known with substantial certainty that contact would result when the trailer was removed.

II. Assault: Bill has a right to be free from the reasonable apprehension of imminent harmful or offensive contact. This right is protected under the tort of assault.

A. Awareness: In order to have apprehension of a contact, one must be aware that it will occur. Since Bill was protesting the removal of his trailer as it was being pulled away, it is likely that he was aware of the actions of The Finance Company and the possibility that he might fall and make contact with the ground.

B. Intent: Once it is proven that the agents of The Finance Company committed a battery, their intent requirement for assault is satisfied; the intent requirement for assault may be satisfied by the intent to commit a battery.

III. Damages for Assault and Battery: Bill may recover damages for his pain and suffering, and the expenses related to his broken leg and hospitalization. Punitive damages may also be awarded if the court considers the conduct of The Finance Company's agents to have been extreme and outrageous.

IV. Infliction of Emotional Distress

A. Intentional: Jane has the right to be free from severe emotional distress that is intentionally or recklessly caused by another's extreme and outrageous conduct. Though the taking of Jane's home and the injuring of her protesting husband may have been extreme and outrageous conduct, and Jane's distress was severe, as evidenced by her need for medical attention, it is doubtful that the agents of The Finance Company acted intentionally or recklessly with respect to Jane since she was not present when the trailer was dispossessed. Thus, relief for the intentional infliction of emotional distress is very unlikely.

B. Negligent: It is unlikely that Jane could recover for the negligent infliction of emotional distress. Relief for this tort is usually only granted if the plaintiff witnessed the accident, the defendant knew of the plaintiff's presence, and the plaintiff was a close relative to the injured party. Even though Jane is Bill's wife, she will not likely recover because she did not witness Bill's injury and was not within the vicinity of the accident. Rather, she developed her emotional distress after hearing about the incident.

V. Trespass to Chattel: Bill and Jane have a right to be free from interference with their possessory interest in the trailer, their chattel. One may commit trespass to chattel by damaging or dispossessing another of a chattel. The denting and dispossessing of the trailer by The Finance Company's agents is most likely a trespass. The fact that Bill and Jane have only paid a down payment for the trailer and consequently do not have title is irrelevant since a person with either constructive or actual possession of the chattel may bring an action for trespass. Further, the fact that The Finance Company acted under a mistaken belief as to the owner of the trailer is not a valid defense to trespass to chattel. Bill and Jane would be entitled to the return of the trailer and its contents, the cost of repairing the trailer's dent, and the fair rental value of the trailer for the time that it was dispossessed.

VI.   Conversion: Bill and Jane have a right to recover the full value of their chattel if another intentionally exercises dominion over the chattel, causing very serious interference with their possessory right such that title actually passes to the interfering party. Although The Finance Company's dispossession and placement of the trailer on sale may be an interference serious enough to constitute conversion, Bill and Jane probably would not want a "forced sale" of their trailer since it was a unique chattel specially designed for them. However, since they have already spent $5000 to replace the contents of the trailer, they will likely claim that the trailer's contents were converted in order to recover their full value, as opposed to the contents themselves which would be available in a suit for trespass.

Note: Though the assault, battery, trespass and conversion were committed by agents of The Finance Company, The Finance Company may be vicariously liable for the torts of their employees.

QUESTION 5

When Harry entered a main highway without looking to see if it was safe, he collided with Jane, who was driving an automobile rented from Ace Auto Rentals (Ace). Jane would have been able to avoid the collision, except that she was driving at a recklessly high speed. Unknown to Ace, Jane did not have a driver's license.

Harry's car caught fire. Dick, a passenger who was sharing expenses and driving responsibilities while on a cross-country trip, escaped without injury. Harry was trapped in the burning car. Tom, a bystander, was severely burned when he tried to pull Harry out of the car. Harry died from his burns several minutes later.

1. What are Tom's rights, if any, against:

    A. Ace? Discuss.

    B. Dick? Discuss.

    C. Harry's estate? Discuss.

2. What are Harry's decedents' rights, if any, against Jane?
    Discuss.

ISSUE/FACT LADDER

Issue	Facts
Paragraph 1 Vicarious Liability	An automobile owned by Ace Auto Rentals was rented to and driven by Jane.
Paragraph 1 Negligence / Contributory Negligence	Harry entered a main highway without looking to see if it was safe.
Paragraph 1 Negligence / Last Clear Chance	Jane would have been able to avoid the collision if she had not been driving at a recklessly high speed.
Paragraph 1 Violation of Statute	Jane was driving at a recklessly high speed. Jane did not have a driver's license.
Paragraph 2 Joint Enterprise	Dick, a passenger, was sharing expenses and driving responsibilities while on a cross-country trip.
Paragraph 2 Rescue	Tom, a bystander, tried to pull Harry out of the car.
Paragraph 2 Damages	Tom was severely burned.
Paragraph 2 Damages	Harry's car caught fire. Harry died from his burns several minutes later.

OUTLINE OF ISSUES

I. Tom v. Ace Auto Rentals

    A. Vicarious Liability

    B. Negligent Entrustment

       1. Duty

       2. Breach

       3. Causation

II. Tom v. Dick

    Joint Enterprise

    A. Right of Control

    B. Common Pecuniary Purpose

    C. Extent of Liability

III. Tom v. Harry's Estate

    Negligence

    A. Duty

    B. Breach

    C. Causation

    D. Damages

IV. Harry's Estate v. Jane

    A. Survival Statutes

    B. Wrongful Death Statutes

    C. Negligence

1. Violation of Statute

2. Contributory Negligence / Last Clear Chance

3. Comparative Negligence

SUBSTANTIVE ANSWER

I. Tom v. Ace Auto Rentals

A. Vicarious Liability: The majority of courts hold that the mere existence of a bailment does not create vicarious liability on the part of a bailor. However, some courts have "automobile consent statutes" that hold the owner of a car vicariously liable for the negligence of any person using the car with the owner's consent. Ace Auto Rentals (Ace) will only be vicariously liable for Jane's negligence if they resided within a jurisdiction that had an automobile consent statute.

B. Negligent Entrustment: Ace may be held responsible for negligently entrusting a potentially dangerous instrument to Jane if Ace breached a duty of care, causing damages to Tom.

1. **Duty:** Ace owes a general duty of care to ascertain whether the people it rents automobiles to are reasonably capable of operating these vehicles.

2. **Breach:** Ace breached its duty of care when it rented an automobile to Jane without ascertaining whether she possessed a valid driver's license.

3. **Causation:** "But for" Ace's unreasonable rental of a car to Jane, the entire accident would not have occurred and Tom would not have been injured attempting the rescue. Ace will probably argue it was not the proximate cause of Tom's injuries. First, there was Jane's reckless driving. This is not a superseding cause because it was foreseeable that Jane might drive recklessly especially since she did not possess a driver's license. Second, there was Harry's negligent driving. Even if this is unforeseeable, most courts find that an unforeseeable intervention is not a superseding cause if it leads to the same type of harm risked by the negligence of the first party. In this case, the harm caused by Harry's negligence, the car accident, is the same type risked by Ace renting a car to a driver without a driver's license. Third, there was Tom's rescue attempt. This is not a superseding cause because the courts treat a rescue attempt as foreseeable unless it is attempted in a grossly careless manner. The rescue was not committed in a grossly careless manner in this case. Therefore, Ace is the proximate cause of Tom's injuries.

II. Tom v. Dick

Joint Enterprise: Tom must prove that Dick was engaged in a joint enterprise with Harry, and is therefore vicariously liable for any injuries caused by Harry.

A. Right of Control: For an activity to be considered a joint enterprise, both parties must have mutual right of control over the enterprise. If Dick and Harry both had say over how the car was driven (e.g., how fast the car was to travel), it is likely that this requirement will be met.

B. Common Pecuniary Purpose: A second requirement for a joint enterprise is a common pecuniary purpose. Many courts hold that the mere sharing of expenses does not constitute a common business purpose. While their general purpose of reaching a destination is related, they are considered to be pursuing independent business interests. Some courts, however, have automobile guest statutes which make the passenger vicariously liable for the actions of the driver. Dick's liability will depend on which view the court utilizes.

C. Extent of Liability: If Dick is found to have been engaged in a joint enterprise with Harry, he will be vicariously liable for all the injuries which Tom sustained as a result of Harry's negligence.

III.   Tom v. Harry's Estate

Negligence: For an action to be brought under negligence, Tom must prove duty, breach of duty, causation and damages. The fact that Harry is deceased will not prevent Tom from bringing this action against his estate.

A. Duty: Harry had a duty, as a driver of an automobile, to exercise reasonable care when driving. This would include observing surrounding traffic conditions.

B. Breach: A reasonable driver would have checked the flow of traffic before entering a main highway. Since Harry failed to do so, he breached his duty to exercise reasonable care when driving.

C. Causation: "But for" Harry's failure to look, the accident and rescue attempt would not have happened. Harry's estate may argue that Tom's rescue attempt was a superseding cause. However, this argument is unlikely to succeed because the courts generally treat a rescue attempt as a foreseeable and natural consequence of an accident unless it is attempted in a grossly careless manner. Thus, Harry is the proximate cause of Tom's injuries.

D. Damages: Harry's estate would be liable for all damages that Harry would be liable for if he were still alive.

IV.   Harry's Estate v. Jane

A. Survival Statutes: Survival statutes allow a decedent's family to recover for the decedent's pain and suffering before death. Since Harry died almost instantaneously, his family would not be able to recover these damages. Furthermore, most states do not allow the use of these statutes to extend to causes of action for damages to real or personal property. Harry's wife, however, may still be able to recover for the damages to the car because she will probably be considered a co-owner.

B. Wrongful Death Statutes: Wrongful death statutes allow a decedent's survivors to assert an action for damages based on the decedent's death. Harry's family should be able to recover damages that occurred after his death, such as loss of future income and loss of companionship.

C. Negligence: Harry's estate would argue that it was Jane's negligence which caused the accident. In the majority of courts, a statutory violation is negligence per se. Thus, if Harry's estate can prove that Jane violated a statute, they will not have to prove there was a duty, breach, or causation. In the minority of courts, a statutory violation is only partial evidence of negligence. The degree of Jane's liability will depend upon whether the courts recognize the doctrines of contributory or comparative negligence.

1. Violation of Statute: Jane violated the speed limit by driving at a recklessly high speed. The violation of this statute is applicable to prove liability if three elements exist. First, that Harry, another driver, was part of the class of persons that the speed limit intended to protect. Second, that the injuries from the car accident were the type of harm the speed limit intended to prevent. Finally, that the required standard of conduct, driving within the speed limit, was clearly defined in the statute. Since these three elements existed, Jane was negligent. Jane will not be able to argue that her statutory duty was excused; compliance with the statute was not more dangerous than noncompliance, she was not faced with an emergency, and compliance was possible. This same analysis could be used to argue that Jane was negligent in violating the statute which requires all drivers to have a valid driver's license.

2. Contributory Negligence / Last Clear Chance: Jane will argue that Harry was contributorily negligent because he entered the main highway without looking. A contributorily negligent plaintiff is barred from recovery. Harry's estate, however, may employ the last clear chance doctrine as a defense. Under this doctrine, a contributorily negligent plaintiff is not barred from recovery if the defendant had the last clear chance to avoid causing the accident. Since Jane could have avoided the accident if she had not been driving at a recklessly high speed, Harry's estate will not be barred from recovering even if he was contributorily negligent.

3. Comparative Negligence: Under the doctrine of comparative negligence, the apportionment of liability between a plaintiff and a defendant is based on their relative degrees of fault. The minority view would allow Harry's estate to recover damages from Jane even if Harry was more at fault in causing the accident. Under the majority view, however, Harry's estate will only recover if he was equally or less negligent than Jane (i.e., 50% or less liable for causing the accident).

QUESTION 6

Patrick carelessly left his wallet containing $100 in Rachel's restaurant and walked away. Rachel observed the wallet, but   neglected to call it to Patrick's attention. Immediately thereafter, David, another restaurant patron, paid his bill and picked up Patrick's wallet by mistake, thinking it was his own.

As David was leaving the restaurant, Patrick saw the wallet in David's hand and recognized it as his own. Before Patrick could call out, David boarded a cable car owned by Trolco. As Patrick boarded the cable car, it pulled away from its stop, causing him to skin his knee. Once aboard, Patrick yelled, "Stop, thief!" and then worked his way around other passengers to where David stood.

The loud accusation angered David, who, even after he noted that the wallet was not his own, retorted, "Don't you call me a thief! Take your wallet and get out of here." He hurled the wallet at Patrick. It struck his face, glanced off, and flew out of the cable car. By the time Patrick was able to get off the cable car, he was unable to find his wallet.

1. What are Patrick's rights, if any, against:

   A. Rachel? Discuss.

   B. David? Discuss.

   C. Trolco? Discuss.

2. What are David's rights, if any, against Patrick? Discuss.

ISSUE/FACT LADDER

Issue	Facts
Paragraph 1 Contributory Negligence	Patrick carelessly left his wallet lying on the counter of Rachel's restaurant and walked away.
Paragraph 1 Negligence / Affirmative Duty	Rachel observed the wallet but neglected to call it to Patrick's attention.
Paragraph 1 Conversion	David, another restaurant patron, picked up Patrick's wallet, thinking it was his own.
Paragraph 2 Negligence	As Patrick boarded the cable car, it pulled away from its stop, causing him to skin his knee.
Paragraph 2 Defamation	Patrick yelled "Stop thief!" to David and worked his way around other passengers to where David stood.
Paragraph 3 Assault and Battery	David retorted, "Take your wallet and get out of here." He then hurled the wallet at Patrick. The wallet struck Patrick's face.
Paragraph 3 Conversion	The wallet flew out of the cable car and Patrick was unable to locate it.

OUTLINE OF ISSUES

I. What are Patrick's rights, if any, against:
A. Rachel? Discuss.
B. David? Discuss.
C. Trolco? Discuss.
II. What are David's rights, if any, against Patrick? Discuss.

I. Patrick v. Rachel

A. Negligence

1. Duty

2. Breach

3. Causation and Damages

B. Defenses

1. Contributory Negligence / Last Clear Chance

2. Comparative Negligence

II. Patrick v. David

A. Conversion

B. Battery

1. Harmful or Offensive Contact

2. Intent to Make Contact

3. Damages

C. Assault

III.   Patrick v. Trolco

Negligence

A. Duty

B. Breach

C. Causation and Damages

IV.   David v. Patrick

Defamation

SUBSTANTIVE ANSWER

I. Patrick v. Rachel

Patrick could bring an action against Rachel under the theory of negligence, but might not prevail due to a possible lack of duty.

A. Negligence: To prevail in a suit under the theory of negligence Patrick must show that Rachel owed him a duty of care, and that Rachel breached the duty of care, causing him damages.

1. Duty: Rachel's failure to inform Patrick that he left his wallet on the restaurant's counter may be regarded as nonfeasance, as opposed to misfeasance. Because an affirmative duty to act only arises if there is a special relationship between the parties, whether Rachel had a duty to take steps to inform Patrick about his wallet depends on their relationship. Courts have often found a legal duty to act if the parties have a business relationship. Because Patrick was a patron of Rachel's restaurant the court may find a business relationship which imposed an affirmative duty on Rachel. However, the relationship may have ended after Patrick paid his bill. Therefore, Rachel's duty will hinge on the court's determination of the duration of her business relationship with Patrick.

2. Breach: If Rachel had an affirmative duty to protect Patrick, it is questionable as to whether she breached it. An affirmative duty to protect one from danger or harm does not necessarily require the protection of another from the loss of property. Because Patrick was not in personal peril, Rachel may not have breached her duty to protect him.

3. Causation and Damages: Whether the failure to inform Patrick about his wallet was the proximate cause of his damages hinges on the foreseeability of David's intervening act of taking the wallet, and the foreseeability of the type of harm suffered by Patrick. Assuming David's act of taking the wallet was negligent, it does not break the chain of causation since negligence by a third party is generally considered foreseeable. Even if David's intervention is not regarded as foreseeable, the harm incurred by the loss of the wallet is of the same type as that risked by Rachel's original failure to act, and Rachel's failure to act would still be regarded as the proximate cause of the loss of the wallet. However, the failure to safeguard the wallet is not the proximate cause of the skinned knee or any injuries which resulted from the wallet being thrown in Patrick's face since these are not foreseeable results of Rachel's failure to act. Thus, Patrick could only recover for the loss of the wallet.

B. Defenses

1. Contributory Negligence / Last Clear Chance: If Patrick brings his suit in a state which bars recovery to a plaintiff who is contributorily negligent, Rachel may contend that Patrick's carelessness in leaving his wallet on the counter bars him from recovering. However, Patrick may still recover since Rachel was aware that Patrick left his wallet behind, and had the last clear chance to safeguard the wallet by returning it.

2. Comparative Negligence: If Patrick's suit is brought in a jurisdiction which applies the doctrine of comparative negligence, Patrick's recovery will be reduced by the percentage of which his negligence caused his loss. If, however, the state has a partial comparative negligence system, Patrick will be barred from recovering if his negligence exceeded Rachel's.

II. Patrick v. David

A. Conversion: Conversion is an intentional exercise of dominion or control over a chattel which so seriously interferes with a plaintiff's right of possession that the plaintiff is entitled to recover the full value of the chattel. While a mistake in good faith as to possession is not a defense to trespass to chattel, it may relieve one of liability for conversion. In addition to good faith, the factors considered in distinguishing a trespass from conversion are the degree of control over the chattel, the amount of damage done to the chattel, and the amount of inconvenience and expense to the original owner of the chattel. Although David originally took the wallet in good faith, this good faith may have dissipated when he decided to hurl the wallet at Patrick on the cable car. Further, the amount of harm and inconvenience to Patrick when David took the wallet, and when he subsequently threw it out the window, weigh very heavily in finding conversion. Thus, it is likely that Patrick would recover for David's conversion of the wallet and its contents.

B. Battery: Patrick had a right to be free from harmful or offensive contact. This right is protected under the tort of battery.

1. Harmful or Offensive Contact: By throwing the wallet at Patrick, David caused it to make harmful contact with Patrick's face. The fact that David did not touch Bill himself is irrelevant, since the harmful or offensive contact of a battery may be inflicted either directly or indirectly.

2. Intent: In order to have committed a battery, David must have either intended that the wallet come in contact with Patrick, or have known with substantial certainty that the contact would result. Because David said "Take your wallet," and hurled it at David, instead of tossing it to David, a reasonable jury might infer that he had the requisite intent to commit a battery.

3. Damages: Patrick may recover any actual damages caused by the wallet hitting his face, and may recover nominal damages if no actual damages resulted. Punitive damages may also be awarded if David's conduct is considered to have been extreme and outrageous.

C. Assault: Patrick had a right to be free from reasonable apprehension of imminent harmful or offensive contact. This right is protected under the tort of assault. It is reasonable that Patrick might have felt apprehension when he saw David hurl the wallet. It is also clear that David had the present ability to cause the apprehended battery with the wallet. Once it is proven that David committed a battery, his intent requirement for assault is satisfied since this requirement may be satisfied by the intent to commit a battery. If David's conduct was extreme and outrageous, punitive damages may be awarded in addition to actual or nominal damages.

III.   Patrick v. Trolco

Negligence: Patrick would likely prevail in a negligence suit against Trolco.

A. Duty: The cable car driver had a duty to act as a reasonably prudent person would to avoid an unreasonable risk of harm to his passengers. The relationship between a common carrier and its passenger has traditionally imposed a further duty on the common carrier to affirmatively assist patrons who are in danger.

B. Breach: Since the cable car driver should have been aware of the boarding and exiting of passengers, the driver breached its duty to Patrick when it started to move the cable car before Patrick was securely aboard. Because of the driver's affirmative duty to protect its passengers, the driver may also be negligent for not assisting Patrick with his injuries, and not assisting him to apprehend David if it was apparent to the driver that David posed an unreasonable risk to Patrick.

C. Causation and Damages: Patrick's skinned knee was proximately caused by the negligence of the driver in moving the car prematurely. The damage was both direct and foreseeable. Since the driver's negligence was the proximate cause of the skinned knee, Patrick should be able to recover these damages from Trolco, which is vicariously liable for its employees. Patrick would not be able to recover for the loss of the wallet and its contents.

IV.   David v. Patrick

Defamation: David has a right not to have his reputation diminished by the acts of another. This right is protected by the tort of defamation. David will assert that Peter's statement "Stop, thief!" was a defamatory statement and that the publication to all the cable car riders damaged his reputation. Because the defamatory statement was oral, it is slander. Although recovery for slander normally requires proof of special damages, an imputation of criminality is slander per se and damages are presumed.

QUESTION 7

White, a Marine Corps officer, was convicted of murder in 1946 in a highly publicized trial. The only evidence against him at the trial was the testimony of Bill and Ted, two former Marines, who claimed that Japanese prisoners of war had been killed while in the custody of White's troops. In 1961, Bill confessed that he and Ted had lied at the trial of White to avoid punishment for their own misconduct. When an investigation confirmed the truth of the confession, White received a pardon and was released from prison.

Shortly after his release from prison, White entered a religious order where he lived in seclusion for the next thirty years. Late in 1991, White developed a serious illness which forced him to leave the order and enter a hospital for treatment.

The News, a daily newspaper in the city in which the hospital is located, has prepared an article that fully and truthfully recounts the trial, imprisonment, and events leading to the pardon of White. The article is based solely on information obtained from public records. *The News* has notified White that it intends to publish the article. White objects to its publication and the prospect of unwelcome publicity. *The News* has also been warned by White's doctors that the emotional stress White may suffer if the story is published will impede his recovery.

If the article is published, on what theory or theories might White base an action for damages against *The News*? Discuss.

ISSUE/FACT LADDER

Issue	Facts
Paragraph 1 Legitimate Public Interest	White, a Marine Corps officer, was convicted of murder in 1946 in a highly publicized trial.
Paragraph 2 Removal From the Public Eye	Shortly after his release from prison, White entered a religious order where he lived in seclusion for the next thirty years.
Paragraph 3 Defamation / Invasion of Privacy	*The News* has prepared a feature article that recounts the trial, imprisonment, and events leading to the pardon of White.
Paragraph 3 Truth as a Defense to Defamation	The article fully and truthfully recounts the trial, imprisonment, and events leading to the pardon of White.
Paragraph 3 Report of the Public Record	The article is based solely on information obtained from public records.
Paragraph 3 Intentional Infliction of Emotional Distress	White objects to its publication and the prospect of unwelcome publicity. *The News* has also been warned by White's doctors that the emotional stress White may suffer if the story is published will impede his recovery.

OUTLINE OF ISSUES

If the story is published, on what theory or theories might White base an action for damages against *The News*? Discuss.

I. Invasion of Privacy

   A. Intrusion Upon Seclusion

   B. Public Disclosure of Private Facts

   C. False Light

II. Defamation

III. Intentional Infliction of Emotional Distress

   A. Intent

   B. Severe Emotional Damage

   C. Extreme and Outrageous Conduct

   D. Damages

SUBSTANTIVE ANSWER

I. Invasion of Privacy: If the article is published, White could bring an action for invasion of privacy under the theories of intrusion upon seclusion, public disclosure of private facts and false light. However, it is unlikely he would prevail under any theory for the invasion of privacy.

A. Intrusion Upon Seclusion: White has a right to be free from intrusion upon the solitude and seclusion of his private life and affairs. In preparing the article, *The News* relied solely on information obtained from public records. Therefore, it appears that there has been no intrusion into White's right to be alone, since White has not been approached or harassed by *The News* in their preparation of the article.

B. Public Disclosure of Private Facts: White has a right to be free from the public disclosure of private facts about his life. *The News*, however, will not be liable for its disclosure of White's ordeal. The information in the article is already a matter of public knowledge. *The News* relied solely on information obtained from public records and, therefore, did not actually disclose any private facts. Furthermore, the subject matter is newsworthy and of legitimate public concern. Thus, *The News* is privileged even if some of the facts were considered private. Although the events occurred over thirty years ago, they remain privileged as long as the information is of public interest.

C. False Light: White has a right to be free from publicity which places him in a false light. Since the information supplied in the article was true and paints an image that would not be objectionable to a reasonable person, White will be unable to recover against *The News* for false light.

II. Defamation: White may also bring an action for defamation against *The News*. However, this action would fail since the article fully and truthfully recounts the trial, imprisonment, and events leading to the pardon of White. Truth is an absolute defense to defamation.

III.   Intentional Infliction of Emotional Distress: White may also bring an action against *The News* for the intentional infliction of emotional distress. White would have to prove that *The News* intentionally or recklessly caused him severe emotional damage through extreme and outrageous conduct.

A. Intent: White must prove that *The News* intended to inflict the distress or knew with substantial certainty that the distress would result. *The News* was warned by White's doctors that the emotional stress White would suffer if the story were published would impede his recovery. Therefore, by disregarding this warning, *The News* had the necessary intent to commit this tort.

B. Severe Emotional Damage: White must also prove that the emotional damage he suffered was severe. Given that White's doctors believe his recovery from a serious illness will be impeded by the emotional stress he will suffer upon publication of the article, it is likely the court will find that these physical manifestations of the distress illustrate the severity of the distress.

C. Extreme and Outrageous Conduct: *The News'* conduct will most likely be seen as extreme and outrageous. They were informed of the serious consequences White would suffer if the article were published, but chose to recklessly disregard these warnings and publish the article. While the story may be of public interest, there is no substantial gain in publishing the article, especially when it is balanced against White's health. Therefore, the conduct exceeded the bounds of decency of a civilized society.

D. Damages: White will be able to recover any actual damages that he can prove. These damages do not necessarily have to be physical damages. White will also probably be able to recover punitive damages.

QUESTION 8

A storage shed on the suburban yard of Construction Co. (Conco) caught fire on a Sunday morning. Dennis, Conco's draftsman at its downtown office, happened to be bicycling by on a personal errand. He broke into the yard office through a closed window and notified the local volunteer fire department. He next located ignition keys and moved eight pieces of heavy equipment onto an adjacent field. The heavy equipment consisted of trucks and bulldozers which were threatened with imminent destruction, but were not damaged.

Unknown to Dennis, the adjacent field belonged to a wholesale florist, Frank. Although the field appeared vacant and unused, Frank had planted it with valuable tulip bulbs. Bulbs valued at $9,000 were destroyed under the weight of the heavy equipment.

After firefighters extinguished the fire, Frank asked Dennis to come to his office to discuss the damage. Dennis agreed. As soon as Dennis entered the office, Frank told Dennis, in the presence of four of Frank's employees, that Dennis would have to remain at the office until he summoned the president of Conco and the president had arrived at the office. When the president arrived an hour later, Frank told Dennis he could leave, and Dennis left.

1. What are Frank's rights against:

   A. Dennis? Discuss.

   B. Conco? Discuss.

2. What are Dennis' rights against Frank? Discuss.

ISSUE/FACT LADDER

Issue	Facts
Paragraph 1 Respondeat Superior/ Vicarious Liability	Dennis, Conco's draftsman, was on a personal errand when he noticed, and acted in response to, the fire.
Paragraph 1 Trespass to Land	Dennis moved eight pieces of heavy equipment onto an adjacent field.
Paragraph 1 Private Necessity	The trucks and bulldozers were threatened with imminent destruction.
Paragraph 2 Damages	Frank's bulbs, valued at $9,000, were destroyed under the weight of the heavy equipment.
Paragraph 3 Consent	Dennis agreed to go to Frank's office to discuss the damages.
Paragraph 3 False Imprisonment	Frank told Dennis, in the presence of four of his employees, that Dennis would have to remain at the office until the president was summoned and arrived.

OUTLINE OF ISSUES

1. What are Frank's rights against:
   A. Dennis? Discuss.
   B. Conco? Discuss.
2. What are Dennis' rights against Frank? Discuss.

I. Frank v. Dennis

   A. Trespass to Land

      1. Physical Invasion

      2. Intent

      3. Damages

   B. Private Necessity

II. Frank v. Conco

   Respondeat Superior / Vicarious Liability

   A. Scope of Employment

   B. Liability for Intentional Torts

III.   Dennis v. Frank

   False Imprisonment

SUBSTANTIVE ANSWER

I. Frank v. Dennis

A. Trespass to Land: Frank has a right to the exclusive possession of his land. This right is protected by the tort of trespass. Frank will sue Dennis for trespass to his tulip garden.

1. Physical Invasion: A physical invasion to another's land occurs if one enters upon, causes another person or object to enter upon, remains upon, or fails to remove something unlawfully upon another's land. By personally entering upon Frank's land with the bulldozers, Dennis has physically invaded Frank's land.

2. Intent: The necessary intent to commit a trespass is the intent to commit or cause the physical invasion of the plaintiff's land. No intent to harm is necessary. Frank clearly had the requisite intent for trespass, since he intended to move the bulldozers onto the adjacent land to avoid their destruction.

3. Damages: Frank would be able to recover both nominal and compensatory damages from Dennis. The fact that the damage to the bulbs was unforeseeable does not preclude Frank from recovering their value, since one is strictly liable for all consequential damages that naturally result from a trespass.

B. Private Necessity: Private necessity provides a privilege to trespass, such that a party who trespasses out of private necessity is only responsible for the actual damages caused by the trespass (as opposed to both nominal and actual damages). The privilege of necessity may be invoked when a party trespasses to avoid injury to oneself, a third party, personal property, or a third party's property. Further, the likelihood and severity of the injury avoided must outweigh the property interest of the party whose land is trespassed upon. Dennis may invoke the privilege of private necessity because he was acting to protect Conco's property from destruction. The fact that complete destruction of the expensive equipment was imminent may be used to show that the prevention of its destruction outweighed Frank's property right at the time. Thus, Dennis was privileged to trespass, and is only liable for the $9,000 in actual damages to Frank's bulb garden.

II. Frank v. Conco

Respondeat Superior / Vicarious Liability: A suit by Frank against Conco would likely hinge on Conco's responsibility for Dennis' tortious conduct. Under the doctrine of respondeat superior, an employer is liable for the torts that employees commit while acting within the scope of employment.

A. Scope of Employment: All actions that are closely connected to an employee's work which are done with a purpose to advance an employer's business interests are within the scope of employment. Even though Dennis was acting to advance his employer's business interest, it is unlikely that the moving of bulldozers was closely connected with his work as a draftsman. Further, Dennis' tort was committed while he was conducting personal errands, lending further support to the proposition that his act was not closely related to his work. Thus, it is questionable that he would be considered to have acted within the scope of his employment.

B. Liability for Intentional Torts: An employer will be liable for an intentional tort committed by an employee with a purpose to advance the employer's business interest. Because Dennis' trespass on Frank's land was an intentional tort, and it was committed to prevent damage to Conco's equipment, Conco will be liable for the damages caused by Dennis' trespass.

III.   Dennis v. Frank

False Imprisonment: Dennis may bring an action for false imprisonment against Frank. However, it is very unlikely that he would prevail. It is unclear from the facts whether any restraint actually existed. Restraint can be accomplished by physical barriers, force, or threats against a person, property, or third person. Perhaps, the door to the office in which Dennis waited was neither closed nor locked. Further, the mere presence of four of Frank's employees does not constitute a threat, absent further evidence of their actions. Dennis may have actually consented to the confinement. Although his express consent was only given to the initial confinement, his consent to remain may be implied if a reasonable person would interpret his failure to object to the confinement as consent. Lastly, if Dennis had knowledge of a reasonable means of escape, he cannot recover for false imprisonment.

QUESTION 9

Harold grows roses in his flower garden. To keep the roses in good health, he applies ROSEBRITE, an insecticide solution regularly manufactured by Acme and sold in spray cans. On several occasions Harold has read a warning printed on the spray can which admonishes:

DO NOT ALLOW THIS SOLUTION TO GET IN EYES OR ON EXPOSED PARTS OF BODY, EXTREMELY TOXIC. DO NOT DRINK. IF CONSUMED, CALL DOCTOR IMMEDIATELY. MANUFACTURER IS NOT LIABLE FOR INJURIES CAUSED BY THIS PRODUCT.

Last week, while Harold was applying ROSEBRITE to the roses, his telephone rang. He left the spray can of ROSEBRITE on the lawn, went inside to answer the phone, and forgot about the ROSEBRITE.

The next day, Johnny, age 5, a neighbor's child who had come over to play with Harold's son, went into the yard, picked up the spray can, and sprayed ROSEBRITE on his arms. He thought the can was filled with perfume because he noticed the picture of roses on the spray can and he could not read. He became ill almost at once.

Johnny's mother had been in the house watching television and had not heard him leave to go see Harold's son. Johnny came into the house crying and was obviously ill. He pointed to the ROSEBRITE spray can and said that the "perfume" made him sick. His mother looked at the spray can and read the warning. Realizing the gravity of the situation, she called an ambulance and got Johnny to the hospital. Johnny suffered cramps, blurred vision, and diarrhea. He was hospitalized for several days.

Though the warning on the spray can did not mention it, washing the exposed area with soap and water would have minimized Johnny's injuries.

1. What are Johnny's rights, if any, against Acme? Discuss.

2. What are Johnny's rights, if any, against Harold? Discuss.

ISSUE/FACT LADDER

Issue	Facts
Paragraph 1 Warning	The warning printed on the can warned against drinking the product or allowing it to get in the eyes or on the body because it was extremely toxic.
Paragraph 1 Disclaimer	The manufacturer expressly disclaimed any liability for injuries caused by the product.
Paragraph 1 Negligence	While Harold was applying Rosebrite, he went to answer his phone and forgot that he left the can on the lawn.
Paragraph 2 Contributory Negligence/ Comparative Negligence	Johnny, a five-year-old, came to play with Harold's son the next day. He picked up the can off the lawn and sprayed Rosebrite on his arms.
Paragraph 2 Adequacy of Warning	Johnny thought the can contained "perfume" because he could not read and saw the picture of roses on the can.
Paragraph 3 Damages	Johnny became ill immediately and was hospitalized for several days with blurred vision, diarrhea and cramps.
Paragraph 3 Contributory Negligence/ Comparative Negligence	Johnny's mother was watching television and did not hear him leave the house.
Paragraph 4 Failure to Warn	The warning on the can failed to mention that washing the exposed area with soap and water would minimize injuries.

OUTLINE OF ISSUES

1. What are Johnny's rights, if any, against Acme? Discuss.
2. What are Johnny's rights, if any, against Harold? Discuss.

I. Johnny v. Acme

   Products Liability Theories

   A. Warranty

   B. Strict Product Liability

      1. Design Defect

      2. Failure to Warn

II. Johnny v. Harold

   A. Negligence

      1. Duty to a Child Trespasser

      2. Breach

      3. Causation

      4. Damages

   B. Contributory Negligence / Comparative Negligence

   C. Ultrahazardous Activities

SUBSTANTIVE ANSWER

I. Johnny v. Acme

Johnny should bring an action against Acme under products liability theories.

A. Warranty: Johnny should claim that Acme breached its implied warranty of merchantability. Acme was a regular seller of Rosebrite and by offering the product for sale it created an implied warranty that it would be fit not only for its intended purposes but also for misuse or abnormal use which was "reasonably foreseeable." It is foreseeable that a user of the product could spray the contents on himself.

Acme would argue that the express disclaimer printed on the can is a defense to a warranty claim. However, for a disclaimer to be valid it must be conspicuous and specifically mention the word "merchantability." Acme's disclaimer is not conspicuous to a young child who cannot read and it also does not meet the latter requirement.

B. Strict Product Liability: Acme, as a manufacturer, is strictly liable if it places a defective product in the market that causes injury to others. Acme may be strictly liable if Johnny can prove that Rosebrite was defectively designed or that Acme failed to warn him of danger of which Johnny should have been aware.

1. Defective Design: Johnny should claim that Acme's product was defectively designed because it lacked a "child proof" safety feature that a reasonable consumer would expect it to have when used in a reasonably foreseeable manner. Johnny might argue that a dangerous pesticide should have the same sort of safety device on it that other common household products have to avoid tampering by curious young children, and that the cost of such a device would be less than the costs of the injuries otherwise suffered.

2. Failure to Warn: Johnny must argue that Acme's warning on the can was inadequate because reasonably foreseeable misusers such as children can not read it. A skull and crossbones illustration would be much more effective, especially as the can had a picture of roses on it which would only encourage children to play with it. In addition, the warning does not convey a fair indication of the nature and gravity of the risks. It only instructs the consumer to call a doctor upon drinking Rosebrite and does not suggest that merely spraying it on oneself, as Johnny did, might require a stay in the hospital. Finally, the warning does not mention that washing the exposed area with soap and water will minimize the injury.

II. Johnny v. Harold

A. Negligence: For an action to be brought under negligence, Johnny must prove duty, breach of that duty, causation, and damages.

1. Duty: A landowner owes a duty of care to children who are known to frequent the area. Harold should have known of Johnny's tendency to enter his land since they were neighbors and Johnny was a friend of Harold's son. In addition, Johnny was unable to appreciate the risk from the insecticide while the dangerous condition created by the insecticide was known or should have been known to Harold, and could have been avoided at only a slight expense.

2. Breach: Harold breached his duty of care to Johnny by leaving the insecticide on the lawn.

3. Causation: "But for" Harold leaving the insecticide on the lawn, Johnny would not have been injured. Harold's act would serve as proximate cause as well because it is reasonably foreseeable that young children would find the can on the front yard and play with it.

4. Damages: As a result of his exposure to Rosebrite, Johnny suffered cramps, blurred vision and diarrhea which led to several days of hospitalization.

B. Contributory Negligence / Comparative Negligence: As Johnny is a child, the standard of care to which he is held is that of a reasonable child with similar age, intelligence and experience. Johnny is not likely to be found negligent as most five year olds cannot read and are not aware of the dangers of a can of insecticide.

Harold may argue as a defense that Johnny's mother was negligent. A mother does have an affirmative duty to protect her child. However, Johnny's mother will argue that she had behaved as a reasonably prudent mother and did not breach that duty when Johnny left the house without her knowledge. Even if Johnny had informed his mother of his intention to visit Harold's son, Johnny still would have found the can of insecticide on the lawn. Even granting a breach of duty, there is no proximate cause because it not foreseeable to a mother that the neighbors, who also have a young child, will leave poisonous substances lying about on the lawn.

C. Ultrahazardous Activities: Johnny may raise the claim that Harold is strictly liable for using insecticide because it involves an inherent and substantial risk of harm. However, spraying the lawn with insecticide is probably not an ultrahazardous activity because the risk of accidents like Johnny's can be eliminated by the exercise of reasonable care. Simply removing the can from the reach of unsuspecting children would have prevented Johnny's injuries.

QUESTION 10

Bayban is an oral contraceptive manufactured by Drugco. Unlike some other birth control pills, it has no known undesirable side effects. However, it is completely ineffective for about 0.4% of all women. Bayban could not be made 100% effective without creating a risk of side effects. Bayban is advertised only through pamphlets mailed to doctors and is sold only on a doctor's prescription. Its label does not mention that it is ineffective with some women, although Drugco so informs the physicians to whom its promotional literature is sent.

Albert and Amy Able had three minor children. Albert's salary, their only source of income, was $28,000 a year and was not likely to increase significantly. In June 1990, Albert and Amy concluded that three children were as many as they could hope to raise and educate adequately. They decided to have no more children. Accordingly, Amy consulted her physician, who prescribed Bayban. She took Bayban regularly until December 1990 when she discovered that she was pregnant.

Since they learned of Amy's pregnancy, the Ables have suffered from severe insomnia caused by economic worries, and as a result Amy has been treated by a psychiatrist. Their 17-year-old daughter, Dora, has also been emotionally upset and under psychiatric treatment since her parents told her that they now could not afford to send her to college.

Amy refused to consider an abortion even though her doctor assured her that it would present no danger to her health. Both the pregnancy and the birth were normal and uneventful. Thomas Able, a healthy baby, was born on August 19, 1991. Thomas was conceived during the time Amy was taking Bayban.

1. What are Amy's rights, if any, against Drugco? Discuss.

2. What are Dora's rights, if any, against Drugco? Discuss.

ISSUE/FACT LADDER

Issue	Facts
Paragraph 1 Design Defect	Bayban was ineffective in 0.4% of all women.
Paragraph 1 Failure to Warn / Learned Intermediary Doctrine	Drugco does not mention on the label of the prescription drug, Bayban, that it is ineffective in some women
Paragraph 2 Damages	Amy became pregnant in December 1990, despite her desire not to have children due to economic reasons.
Paragraph 3 Damages / Negligent Infliction of Emotional Distress	Amy and Dora had been treated by a psychiatrist, and the Ables could no longer afford to send Dora to college.
Paragraph 4 Duty to Mitigate Damages	Amy refused to consider an abortion even though her doctor assured her that it would present no danger to her health.

OUTLINE OF ISSUES

1. What are Amy's rights, if any, against Drugco? Discuss.
2. What are Dora's rights, if any, against Drugco? Discuss.

I. Amy v. Drugco

   A. Products Liability

      1. Strict Products Liability

         a. Design Defect

         b. Failure to Warn

      2. Negligence

      3. Implied Warranty of Fitness for Intended Use

   B. Damages and the Duty to Mitigate

II. Dora v. Drugco

   A. Negligent Infliction of Emotional Distress

   B. Interference with a Prospective Advantage

SUBSTANTIVE ANSWER

I. Amy v. Drugco

A. Products Liability: Amy will likely sue Drugco for products liability under the theories of strict products liability, negligence, and breach of an implied warranty.

1. Strict Products Liability: Amy's strict product liability action will be based on a claim of defective design and the failure to warn.

a. Design Defect: A product has a design defect if either the design's dangers outweigh its utility, or the design does not perform as safely as a reasonable consumer would expect. Because the drug Bayban is effective in 99.6% of all women without producing any adverse side effects, it is unlikely that Amy could prove that the design's dangers outweigh its utility. Further, a reasonable consumer would expect that a contraceptive might not be 100% effective. Lastly, it may be difficult to show that the failure to prevent conception is a lack of safe performance. Thus it is unlikely that Amy would recover under a design defect theory.

b. Failure to Warn: A product may be considered unreasonably dangerous for purposes of strict products liability if it is unaccompanied by adequate warnings of potential product dangers and directions for use. For normal products, the manufacturer's duty to warn extends to the ultimate user or consumer. However, a majority of jurisdictions have developed an exception, known as the learned intermediary rule, which limits a prescription drug manufacturer's duty to warn. Under this doctrine, a prescription drug manufacturer only has a duty to warn the physician, as opposed to the user of the drug. The physician is a learned intermediary who is best able to inform the drug user of all material risks. Because Bayban is a prescription drug, it is likely that Drugco had no duty to warn Amy. However, a few courts have carved out an exception to the exception whereby a manufacturer of a prescription contraceptive has a duty to warn the ultimate user of the contraceptive. This exception is based on the rationale that the patient is actively involved in the decision to use a contraceptive, and, thus, is not dependent on the physician for advice. If Amy brings her suit for failure to provide adequate warning in one of these jurisdictions, she could recover.

2. Negligence: Actions for design defect and failure to warn may also be brought under a negligence theory. Under an analysis similar to that given above, Amy will not recover for a design defect, but may recover for the failure to warn if she brings the suit in a jurisdiction that extends a contraceptive manufacturer's duty to warn to the ultimate consumer.

3. Implied Warranty of Fitness for Intended Use: Amy may also try to bring an action claiming that Drugco breached an implied warranty of fitness for intended use.

She would have to argue that its intended use was the prevention of pregnancy, she used the drug according to proper instructions, and her pregnancy resulted because the drug was unfit for its purpose. However, she may not prevail if the court finds a broader purpose to the drug; a purpose to provide the greatest amount of contraceptive effectiveness with the least amount of side effects. Perhaps this contraceptive pill was intended for use by women who are highly susceptible to side effects and who are thus willing to accept the 0.4% risk of pregnancy in light of the certainty that side effects will not result. If this is the case, the product is fit for its intended use, and Amy cannot recover under this theory.

B. Damages and the Duty to Mitigate: Most courts have limited recovery for damages caused by faulty contraception to pain and suffering, and medical expenses related to the unwanted pregnancy. A few courts, however, have allowed recovery of the costs of raising the unwanted child, offset by the financial and emotional benefits derived from the child. In such a case, there is no duty to mitigate damages through an abortion since there is only a duty to avoid injuries which a reasonable person would have avoided, and a reasonable person might not find abortion a reasonable alternative to pregnancy for various ethical reasons.

II. Dora v. Drugco

A. Negligent Infliction of Emotional Distress: Dora may try to recover for the emotional distress she suffered when her parents told her that they could not afford to send her to college due to the added expense of raising Thomas. Unless Dora can prove that she is a foreseeable plaintiff she cannot recover from Drugco for negligent infliction of emotional distress. Further, it is unclear whether Drugco is the proximate cause of Dora's distress. It was not the conception and birth of Thomas that caused her distress, but rather her parents' decision that their funds should be reallocated in such a way that Dora could no longer attend college. Because her parents' actions break the chain of causation between Drugco and Dora's mental distress, it is unlikely that she could recover from Drugco under this theory.

B. Interference with a Prospective Advantage: Dora may try to recover the cost of her education under a theory of interference with prospective advantage. She probably will not recover because there was no intentional interference; Drugco did not induce Amy and Albert to reallocate their funds so as to deprive Dora of financing for her college education.

QUESTION 11

Phil, a dignified insurance salesman and president of several civic organizations, was walking down Ribbon Lane when he noticed that his shoelace was untied. When he stooped down to retie it, his photograph was snapped by Lorraine, a commercial photographer.

Lorraine takes pictures of people on public sidewalks while they are unaware of what is happening. She then hands each person a ticket bearing a serial number that corresponds to the number on the exposed film of the picture taken. The holder can then mail the ticket to Lorraine's studio with ten dollars, and receive a print of the photograph. Otherwise, the undeveloped film is destroyed.

When Phil was handed his ticket, he threw it on the sidewalk. The next passerby was Robert, a wealthy socialite and friend of Phil. His picture was also taken by Lorraine. Robert accidentally dropped his ticket. When he attempted to retrieve it, he picked up Phil's discarded ticket by mistake. Thinking it was his own, Robert filled the ticket out and sent it to Lorraine's studio with ten dollars. Lorraine mailed him the corresponding picture in a sealed envelope.

The picture of Phil which Robert received gave the appearance that Phil was reaching down to pick up a discarded cigar butt on the sidewalk. Robert was highly amused at the picture, and posted it on the bulletin board at the country club to which both he and Phil belonged. The picture quickly became the subject of hilarious conversation among the members. Finally, one member of the country club who was the editor of *Town Talk*, a local paper, removed the picture and published it in the hobby section of the paper in connection with an article entitled: "Can you trust your camera?"

1. What are Phil's rights, if any, against Lorraine? Discuss.

2. What are Phil's rights, if any, against Robert? Discuss.

3. What are Phil's rights, if any, against *Town Talk*? Discuss.

ISSUE/FACT LADDER

Issue	Facts
Paragraph 1 Public Figure	Phil was a dignified insurance salesman and president of several civic organizations.
Paragraph 2 Intrusion Upon Seclusion	Lorraine takes pictures of people while they walk down public side walks.
Paragraph 3 Publication / Appropriation	Lorraine mailed Robert the corresponding picture in a sealed envelope.
Paragraph 4 Defamation / False Light	The picture gave the appearance that Phil was reaching down to pick up a discarded cigar butt on the sidewalk.
Paragraph 4 Publication	Robert posted the picture on the bulletin board at the country club to which both he and Phil belonged.
Paragraph 4 Publication / Appropriation	One member of the country club who was the editor of Town Talk, a local paper, published the picture in the hobby section of the paper.

OUTLINE OF ISSUES

1. What are Phil's rights, if any, against Lorraine? Discuss.
2. What are Phil's rights, if any, against Robert? Discuss.
3. What are Phil's rights, if any, against *Town Talk*? Discuss.

I. Phil v. Lorraine

    A. Invasion of Privacy

        1. Intrusion Upon Seclusion

        2. Appropriation

        3. False Light

    B. Defamation

II. Phil v. Robert

    A. False Light

    B. Defamation

III.   Phil v. *Town Talk*

    A. Invasion of Privacy

        1. Appropriation

        2. False Light

    B. Defamation

SUBSTANTIVE ANSWER

I. Phil v. Lorraine

A. Invasion of Privacy: Phil could bring an action against Lorraine for invasion of privacy under the theories of intrusion upon seclusion, appropriation and false light.

1. Intrusion Upon Seclusion: Phil has a right to be free from intrusion upon the solitude and seclusion of his private life and affairs. It is unlikely that Phil could recover against Lorraine for intrusion upon seclusion since the picture she took of Phil occurred while he was walking down a public sidewalk. The intrusion must be into a private place to be actionable. Furthermore, the intruder must have the intent to harm the person. Lorraine did not intend to harm Phil; the harm that occurred was accidental.

2. Appropriation: Appropriation involves the use of a person's name or likeness for the commercial advantage of another without receiving the person's permission. Phil could argue that Lorraine used his picture for a commercial advantage, the selling of the picture. Under normal circumstances this would not be appropriation because the picture is only sold with the person's consent, when they mail in the ticket. However, in this case the picture was sold without Phil's consent because of the mistake that was made. Phil would still probably be unable to recover because his picture was not the inducement for Lorraine and Robert's transaction. Robert purchased the picture because he believed it was his own.

3. False Light: Phil has a right to be free from publicity which places him in a false light. Phil could argue that he was placed in a false light when Lorraine mailed the picture to Robert. However, it is unlikely that this action would fulfill the requirement that the person be placed before the public. Her actions only placed Phil before Robert. The subsequent actions by Robert and *Town Talk* which resulted in Phil being placed before the public could not be foreseen by Lorraine. Therefore, she would not be liable.

B. Defamation: Most courts hold that a defamatory communication embodied in "physical form" is libel. Therefore, Phil's action alleging that the picture was defamatory would be a libel action. Publication would occur when Robert received the picture that Lorraine mailed. Lorraine had the necessary intent to publish the picture since she intentionally mailed the picture to Robert. However, she might argue that Phil is a public figure because of his recognizable position within the community. If that is established Phil will only be able to recover if he can prove that Lorraine published the picture with malice. The success of the action would also turn on whether a jury interprets the picture as portraying Phil in a defamatory manner that detracted from his reputation. If she is found liable, general damages would be presumed because this is an action for libel.

II. Phil v. Robert

A. False Light: Phil has a right to be free from publicity which places him in a false light. Phil could argue that by posting the picture on the bulletin board at the country club, Robert placed Phil before the public in a false light. The picture would be considered to have been placed before the public since the facts stipulate that the picture became the subject of conversation among the members of the club. Therefore, the success of this action will depend on whether a jury believes the image of Phil conveyed by the photograph would be objectionable to a reasonable person. An extra-sensitive plaintiff may not recover.

B. Defamation: Phil's action against Robert for libel relies on the same analysis as for his libel action against Lorraine. The picture would be considered published since it was conveyed to the members of the country club after it was placed on the bulletin board by Robert. He had the necessary intent to publish the picture since he intentionally posted the picture on the bulletin board. The case will turn on whether Phil is considered a public figure, whether Robert published the picture with malice and whether a jury would interpret the picture as defamatory.

III.   Phil v. *Town Talk*

A. Invasion of Privacy: Phil could bring an action against *Town Talk* for invasion of privacy under the theories of appropriation and false light.

1. Appropriation: Appropriation involves the use of a person's name or likeness for the commercial advantage of another without receiving the person's permission. Although *Town Talk* did use the photograph of Phil in its paper, it is unlikely Phil will be able to recover. The majority of courts hold that no appropriation exists where a person's picture is used merely as an illustration for an article (e.g., a picture of a woman next to an article about women). The picture did not identify Phil, but instead was used in connection with an article entitled: "Can you trust your camera?" While newspapers do seek a commercial advantage, it was not Phil's picture that was the basis of this advantage.

2. False Light: Phil has a right to be free from publicity which places him in a false light. Phil could argue that by publishing the picture in their paper, *Town Talk* placed him before the public in a false light. *Town Talk* might claim that they were privileged because they did not publish the picture with malice, but it is unlikely that this defense will succeed, since the picture is not sufficiently newsworthy to invoke that privilege. The success of this action will depend on whether a jury believes that the image the picture painted of Phil would be objectionable to a reasonable person. An extra-sensitive plaintiff may not recover.

B. Defamation: Phil's action against *Town Talk* for libel relies on the same analysis as his libel action against Lorraine. *Town Talk* intentionally published the picture in its newspaper. The case will turn on whether Phil is considered a public figure, whether *Town Talk* published the picture with malice and whether a jury would interpret the picture as defamatory.

QUESTION 12

Abel and Baker were working on a scaffold lawfully erected over a public sidewalk. Abel, contrary to an express rule of his employer, was not wearing a hard hat.

While trying to park her automobile near one of the supports of the scaffold, Diana maneuvered it into such a position that she knew there was a risk of knocking the scaffold down if she backed up without someone to guide her. She appealed for help to Sam, a stranger who was passing by. Sam just laughed. Angered, Diana proceeded to back up her automobile without assistance, and knocked a support out from under the scaffold, causing Abel and Baker to fall.

Abel severely fractured his skull and was taken unconscious to a hospital. If he had been wearing his hard hat, he would have suffered only a slight concussion with minimal disability.

Baker fractured a vertebra, but he was able to walk and felt only slight pain. The fracture could have been easily diagnosed by x-ray, and a medical doctor of average competence could have successfully treated it by immobilization. Instead of visiting a physician, Baker worked the rest of the day. While driving his car home later that day, Baker stopped at an intersection and his car was struck from the rear by a car driven negligently by Ed. The collision caused only slight damage to Baker's car, but was sufficiently severe to aggravate the fracture in Baker's back, resulting in paralysis.

Diana and Sam settled Baker's claim against them and received general releases from him. Abel sued Diana and Sam. Baker sued Ed. Assume that Diana, Sam and Ed raise all appropriate defenses.

1. What are Abel's rights, if any, against:

   A. Diana? Discuss.

   B. Sam? Discuss.

2.   What are Baker's rights, if any, against Ed? Discuss.

ISSUE/FACT LADDER

Issue	Facts
Paragraph 1 Contributory Negligence / Mitigation of Damages	Abel was not wearing his hard hat, contrary to his employer's express rule.
Paragraph 2 Negligence	Although Diana knew there was a risk of knocking down the scaffold if she attempted to back her car up without someone to guide her, she attempted it anyway, causing Abel and Baker to fall.
Paragraph 2 Affirmative Duty	Sam, a stranger, refused Diana's request for help to guide her as she backed up her car.
Paragraph 3 Damages	Abel severely fractured his skull but would have suffered only a slight concussion if he had been wearing his hard hat.
Paragraph 4 Damages / Aggravation of Injuries	Baker fractured a vertebra when he fell from the scaffold, but he did not realize it and did not seek medical attention. Later that day, Baker was stopped at an intersection when his car was struck from the rear by a car driven negligently by Ed. Baker's car was only slightly damaged but the collision aggravated the fracture in Baker's back, resulting in paralysis.

OUTLINE OF ISSUES

1. What are Abel's rights, if any, against:
   A. Diana? Discuss.
   B. Sam? Discuss.
2. What are Baker's rights, if any, against Ed? Discuss.

I. Abel v. Diana

    A. Negligence

        1. Duty

        2. Breach

        3. Causation

        4. Damages / Failure to Mitigate

    B. Contributory Negligence

II. Abel v. Sam

    Affirmative Duty

III. Baker v. Ed

    A. Damages

    B. Contributory Negligence / Comparative Negligence

SUBSTANTIVE ANSWER

I. Abel v. Diana

A. Negligence: For an action to be brought under negligence, Abel must prove duty, breach of that duty, causation and damages.

1. Duty: Diana has the duty to drive as a reasonable person would under the circumstances. A reasonable person would not back up without guidance and knowingly disregard the risk of knocking down the scaffolding.

2. Breach: Diana breached her duty to drive safely when she disregarded the risks and knocked down the scaffold.

3. Causation: "But for" Diana hitting the scaffolding with her car, the scaffolding would not have collapsed and Abel would not have fallen. Proximate causation is established because it was foreseeable that striking the scaffolding would cause it to collapse. Diana herself realized this possibility but decided to ignore it. As scaffolding is designed primarily to support people who are doing work on the exterior of buildings, it is also foreseeable that there would be people on the scaffolding who would be injured in such an accident.

4. Damages / Failure to Mitigate: Abel will seek recovery for medical expenses, lost earnings, future earnings and pain and suffering. Had he worn his hard hat, Abel would have suffered only a slight concussion with minimal disability. Diana will argue that Abel had a duty to mitigate the damages and cannot recover for harm which would have been avoided had he worn his hard hat. Courts have primarily applied the defense of mitigation to actions taken by a plaintiff after the accident but Abel's action of not wearing the hat took place prior to the accident. However, courts have made exceptions for claims involving seat belts and motorcycle helmets. If the court views this claim as analogous to the exceptions for seat belts and motorcycle helmets, Abel's damages may be reduced to what they would have been had he worn the hat. Other courts do not reduce the damages awarded to the plaintiff in cases involving the seat belt or motorcycle exception.

B. Contributory Negligence: The court is unlikely to grant contributory negligence in this situation because it would bar Abel from recovering for any of his injuries even though some injuries would still have resulted had he worn his hard hat. In analogous situations, many courts have considered this result unjust.

II. Abel v. Sam

A. Affirmative Duty: Abel cannot bring a negligence action against Sam because Sam did not have a duty to act for the benefit of Abel. Sam did not put Abel in peril and he did not assume a duty to act. Finally, there was no special relationship between Abel and Sam nor between Sam and Diana.

III.   Baker v. Ed

A. Damages: Ed negligently rear-ended Baker and, thus, is liable for the aggravation of Baker's pre-existing injury. While he is not responsible for Baker's fractured vertebra sustained in his fall from the scaffold, he is liable for the paralysis resulting from the car wreck. Baker may recover for lost earnings, future earnings, pain and suffering, mental distress and property damage.

B. Contributory Negligence: As Baker's car was struck in the rear as it was stopped at an intersection, Baker did not violate his duty to drive safely. Ed may argue that Diana's negligence was the proximate cause of Baker's eventual injury, or that Baker had a duty to seek medical attention after falling from the scaffold. However, these questions are not relevant as neither impacts on the occurrence of the accident. The court is likely to hold that Ed must take the plaintiff as he finds him.

QUESTION 13

Oilco, a corporation engaged in the business of developing oil fields, took seismographic readings under two parcels of land owned by Brett, a farmer, without his knowledge. The method used was to explode small charges of dynamite outside each parcel and determine the speed with which the shock waves passed under the land to a receiving station on a public highway on the other side. In this manner, a trained seismologist could determine with fair accuracy the geologic formation of the terrain and whether oil was likely to be located therein.

As a result of these tests, Oilco decided that there was a good probability that large oil reserves underlay Brett's Parcel One, which consisted of some ponds and open fields, and was used for raising grain. Oilco caused a corporation, The Duck Club, to be formed by three officers of Oilco. The Duck Club purchased Parcel One from Brett, informing him that it wanted to establish a club for duck hunters on the parcel. The price paid was a fair price for farmland, but was far below the value of the property as future oil producing land.

Parcel Two, which was some distance from Parcel One, had extensive farm structures and a water well. The tests indicated that there was no probability of oil and Oilco did nothing further with respect to Parcel Two.

Approximately three months after selling Parcel One, Brett discovered that no club had been established, but that Oilco was drilling for oil. He also discovered that the casing in the water well on Parcel Two was badly cracked and the water well had to be entirely redrilled. At this time, he learned of the seismographic tests that had been made by Oilco. Expert testimony indicated that normally the shock waves from Oilco's tests would not cause any damage to the land or improvements, but because of an unusual soil condition, the shock waves from Oilco's tests caused the damage to Brett's water well.

What are Brett's rights, if any, against Oilco? Discuss.

ISSUE/FACT LADDER

Issue	Facts
Paragraph 1 Trespass to Land	Oilco took seismographic readings under two parcels of land owned by Brett, a farmer, without his knowledge. The method used sent shock waves under the land.
Paragraph 1 Abnormally Dangerous Activity	Oilco exploded small charges of dynamite outside each parcel of land sending shock waves under the land.
Paragraph 2 Vicarious Liability	Oilco caused a corporation, The Duck Club, to be formed by three officers of Oilco.
Paragraph 2 Intentional Misrepresentation	The Duck Club purchased Parcel One from Brett, informing him that it wanted to establish a club for duck hunters on the parcel. In fact, The Duck Club had purchased the land knowing that it would be used by Oilco to drill for oil.
Paragraph 4 Private Nuisance	Brett discovered that the casing in the water well on Parcel Two was badly cracked because of the shock waves from Oilco's tests.
Paragraph 4 Damages	The casing in the water well on Parcel Two was badly cracked and the well had to be entirely redrilled.
Paragraph 4 Extrasensitive Plaintiff	Expert testimony indicated that normally the shock waves from Oilco's tests would not have caused any damage to the land or improvements, but did so because of an unusual soil condition.

OUTLINE OF ISSUES

What are Brett's rights, if any, against Oilco? Discuss.

I. Trespass to Land

    A. Physical Invasion

    B. Intent

    C. Damages

II. Private Nuisance

    A. Substantial Interference

    B. Unreasonable Interference

III.   Strict Liability

IV.   Intentional Misrepresentation

    A. Vicarious Liability

    B. Misrepresentation

    C. Intent and Reliance

SUBSTANTIVE ANSWER

I. Trespass to Land

Brett has a right to the exclusive possession of his land. This right is protected by the tort of trespass. In order for a trespass action to succeed, Brett must prove that there was an intentional physical invasion to his land.

A physical invasion to another's land occurs if a person enters upon the land, causes another person or an object to enter the land, fails to remove something from the land which the person is under a legal duty to remove, or wrongfully remains on the land, despite a legal entry. Most courts recognize trespass that occurs below the surface, although some courts prefer sub-surface trespass to be brought under a nuisance theory. Therefore, by sending shock waves under Brett's land, Oilco physically invaded Brett's land.

A person must also intend to commit or cause the physical invasion of the plaintiff's land. No intent to harm is necessary. Oilco intentionally sent the shock waves through Brett's land. It does not matter that they did not intend to damage the property, or that they could not foresee that damage would occur. Therefore, a trespass has occurred.

Brett would be entitled to recover both nominal and actual damages. Oilco will be held strictly liable for all consequential damages that are the direct and proximate result of the trespass. Expert testimony revealed that the shock waves from Oilco's tests caused the damage to Brett's water well. The fact that the shock waves would not have caused any damage to the land, but for an unusual soil condition, is irrelevant.

II. Private Nuisance

Brett could also argue that Oilco's activities were a private nuisance. Brett would be required to prove that Oilco substantially and unreasonably interfered with his land.

Brett owned both parcels of land at the time of the nuisance and, therefore, has the necessary possessory interest to bring a private nuisance action. However, because the interference must be substantial, Brett will only have a cause of action for Parcel Two. His use and enjoyment of Parcel One was not interfered with by Oilco's tests. Parcel Two, however, received damage to its water well because of the shock waves. Since this parcel contained extensive farming structures, the damage which denied Brett the use of the water well, and caused the need to entirely redrill it, would be considered a substantial interference.

A nuisance must not only be substantial, but also unreasonable for a private nuisance action to be successful. In determining unreasonableness, a court will balance the harm to the plaintiff against the benefits of the defendant's conduct to the community. The harm to Brett is substantial because without a working water well, he will be unable to properly maintain his farm. While the drilling of oil might be seen as a necessary activity that benefits the entire community, the activity in question is Oilco's tests. While testing for oil may be a necessary activity, it is not necessary that these tests be conducted without the consent of the landowners. Performing non-consensual tests does not guarantee that more oil will be produced, or that landowners will cooperate with Oilco to produce oil once the tests are performed. Therefore, the interference is unreasonable and Brett will recover full damages.

III. Strict Liability

Brett could also argue that Oilco is strictly liable for any damages he suffered from their seismographic testing because the activity involves an inherent and substantial risk of harm. In performing the tests, small charges of dynamite were exploded to cause shock waves to run through the land. Most courts have found blasting of dynamite to be an ultrahazardous activity, and have imposed strict liability on those who engage in this activity because of the high probability that serious harm will occur.

Brett is a foreseeable plaintiff because his property, the water well, was damaged by the aftershocks from the detonation of dynamite; it was a result of the kind of risk that made blasting an ultrahazardous activity. The fact that the shock waves would not have caused any damage to the land, except for an unusual soil condition is irrelevant. Oilco is liable for any harm it caused.

IV. Intentional Misrepresentation

Brett could also bring an action against Oilco for intentional misrepresentation in purchasing his land. While it was actually The Duck Club that misrepresented the reason they were purchasing the land, Oilco caused The Duck Club to be formed by three of their officers. Therefore, Oilco is vicariously liable for the action of The Duck Club since the corporation was essentially acting as an agent of Oilco.

There were two types of misrepresentations made to Brett. The first involved The Duck Club's failure to inform Brett that they had run tests and intended to drill for oil on the land. This nondisclosure of material facts would not be actionable, however, because, as a purchaser of land, The Duck Club had no affirmative duty to reveal to Brett, the seller, its intentions regarding the use of the land.

The other misrepresentation occurred when The Duck Club informed Brett that it wanted to establish a club for duck hunters on the land when they really intended to drill for oil. The Duck Club had the necessary intent since it knew that the statement it was making was false. The case will turn on whether The Duck Club intended to induce Brett to rely on the misrepresentation and whether he justifiably relied on the misrepresentation. It appears that The Duck Club did not inform Brett about the oil so as to get a better price for the land. There is no evidence, however, that the misrepresentation as to the future use of the land actually induced Brett to sell the land, or to sell the land at a reduced price. Therefore, unless Brett can prove that he justifiably relied on The Duck Club's misrepresentation in selling or in fixing the price of his land, he will not recover for intentional misrepresentation.

QUESTION 14

Angela took her diamond ring to Frank, a jeweler, to have the stone reset. After Frank had agreed to reset the stone and Angela had left the shop, Frank placed the ring on a counter while he bent down to open a safe underneath. Suddenly, Frank suffered a massive coronary and fell to the floor. Although Frank knew that he had a bad heart condition, he had not had a heart attack for four years. During the commotion Terry, a customer, took Angela's ring and left the shop.

As Terry was leaving the shop, Angela was standing outside and saw him with her ring. When she yelled at him to stop, Terry ran down an alley and Angela chased after him. She realized that she could not catch him and that she would not be able to identify him to the police. As she was running, she noticed a bow and arrow lying on the ground. She picked it up and shot Terry in the leg.

When Terry fell, Angela's ring dropped out of his hand and rolled into the middle of the street. At the same time, a cement paver happened to be rolling down the street. It crushed the ring into the ground, completely destroying it.

Terry was arrested for stealing Angela's ring. As a result of his injury, Terry walks with a permanent limp.

Although the ring was destroyed, Angela had insured the ring only a few hours earlier. The insurance paid for most of the cost of replacing the ring. However, Angela suffered extreme emotional distress over the loss of the ring because it was a family heirloom that was given to her by her great grandmother.

1. What are Angela's rights, if any, against:

   A. Frank? Discuss.

   B. Terry? Discuss.

2. What are Terry's rights, if any, against Angela? Discuss.

ISSUE/FACT LADDER

Issue	Facts
Paragraph 1 Negligence	Frank left Angela's ring on the counter while he tried to open the safe.
Paragraph 1 Damages	Angela's ring was stolen from the jewelry shop.
Paragraph 2 Conversion	Terry stole Angela's ring, substantially interfering with her possession of it.
Paragraph 2 Battery	Angela shot Terry in the leg with a bow and arrow.
Paragraph 3 Negligent Infliction of Emotional Distress	Angela was upset about losing the ring, a family heirloom given to her by her great-grandmother.
Paragraph 4 Damages	Terry now walks with a permanent limp.
Paragraph 5 Collateral Source Rule	Angela's insurance company paid for the cost of replacing the ring.

OUTLINE OF ISSUES

1. What are Angela's rights, if any, against:
   A. Frank? Discuss.
   B. Terry? Discuss.
2. What are Terry's rights, if any, against Angela? Discuss.

I. Angela v. Frank

   Negligence

   1. Duty

   2. Breach

   3. Causation

   4. Damages / Collateral Source Rule

II. Angela v. Terry

   A. Trespass to Chattel

   B. Conversion

   C. Negligent Infliction of Emotional Distress

III.   Terry v. Angela

   A. Battery

      1. Harmful or Offensive Contact

      2. Intent to Make Contact

   B. Recovery of Property

      1. Force

      2. Rightful Wrongdoer

      3. Unlawful Possession

4. In Hot Pursuit

5. Timely Oral Demand

SUBSTANTIVE ANSWER

I. Angela v. Frank

Angela could bring an action against Frank under the theory of negligence. To prevail in this action, Angela would have to show that Frank owed her a duty of care, and that Frank breached that duty, causing her damages.

Angela could argue that Frank had a special relationship with her because of their business relationship. Therefore, he owed her a duty to exercise reasonable care under the circumstances to prevent theft or damage to Angela's ring. To determine the circumstances surrounding an event, most courts include the physical characteristics of the defendant. Thus, the court will ask what a reasonable person with the physical attributes of the defendant would have done. Frank had a bad heart condition and previously had suffered a heart attack. Frank was aware of his condition and would probably be held liable for any damages that were proximately caused by his sudden heart attack. Frank breached his duty to protect Angela's ring from theft by leaving the ring out on the counter because he knew he was prone to heart attacks which could inhibit his ability to protect the ring.

"But for" Frank's negligence in leaving Angela's ring on the counter, the ring never would have been stolen and subsequently destroyed. Frank may try to argue that he was not the proximate cause of the ring being destroyed because although the theft might have been foreseeable, the destruction by the cement paver was not. Thus, this was a superseding cause that relieves Frank's liability. This argument will not be successful because although the manner of the harm was unforeseeable, the type of harm, that Angela would no longer have her ring, was not. Therefore, Frank was the proximate cause of Angela's injuries.

If Angela is successful, she would be able to recover actual damages as well as for the emotional distress of losing the ring, if she can prove that this is severe. The fact that Angela received compensation from her insurance company would not prevent her from recovering against Frank and it would not be used by the jury in determining the damage award. Under the collateral source rule, a tortfeasor may not introduce evidence to prove that a plaintiff has been compensated by an another source, such as insurance.

II.   Angela v. Terry

Angela has a claim against Terry for either trespass to chattels or conversion. Trespass to chattels is the intentional interference with a person's use or possession of property. The defendant does not have to intend harm but must merely intend to do the act which turns out to constitute the interference. The tort of conversion occurs when the defendant so substantially interferes with the plaintiff's possession of her property that it is only fair to require the defendant to pay the property's full value in damages.

Terry intended to steal Angela's ring and Angela's suffered actual damages when the ring was destroyed, making recovery of the property impossible. When determining if a defendant has committed a conversion, the court will examine the extent and duration of the defendant's exercise of control over the item, the defendant's good faith, the harm done and the inconvenience and expense caused to the plaintiff. As a thief, Terry is liable under the doctrine of conversion because he took control of the ring, in bad faith, which led to its destruction. Terry is liable to Angela for the full value of the ring.

Angela may claim that Terry negligently inflicted extreme emotional distress upon her. However, the general rule is that there can be no recovery for negligent infliction of purely emotional harm. Some courts have recognized limited exceptions to this rule, but none of these apply to Angela and the loss of her ring.

III. Terry v. Angela

Terry could sue Angela for battery. Terry has a right to be free from harmful or offensive contact. This right is protected under the intentional tort of battery. To succeed in this action, Terry would have to prove that there was an intentional harmful or offensive touching by Angela to his person.

Terry must prove that the contact was harmful or offensive. This is determined by the reasonable person standard. It seems very likely that a reasonable person would conclude that being shot in the leg by an arrow was harmful contact, especially considering that the contact resulted in a permanent injury to Terry. The fact that Angela did not actually touch Terry is irrelevant. Harmful or offensive contact may be either direct or indirect. Terry must also prove that Angela had the necessary intent to make contact. There is little doubt that Angela intended to make contact with Terry when she aimed the bow and arrow at him.

Angela will probably argue that she was attempting to recover her property, and therefore, the contact was justified. A property owner may use reasonable force to recover any unlawfully taken chattels when the property owner is in hot pursuit of the taker, and the taker refuses to heed an oral demand to return the chattels.

Angela was in immediate pursuit of Terry upon learning that he had her ring. This possession was clearly unlawful since Terry took the ring from Frank's store without any permission. Whether Angela can invoke the privilege to use force to recover property will depend on two factors: if she issued a timely oral demand and if she used reasonable force. While Angela yelled for Terry to stop upon first seeing him with the ring, she did not demand that he stop just before shooting him with the arrow. Angela could argue, however, that such a demand would have been futile, so she did not have to make a second oral demand.

There is also a question whether Angela used reasonable force. Although the force Angela used was not deadly and did not cause serious injury, is was capable of causing serious injury to Terry. Since it is doubtful that Angela was proficient with the bow and arrow, the chances that the arrow would hit Terry in another part of his body and cause serious injury was substantial. Therefore, the court may find that the force used was unreasonable and Angela is barred from invoking the privilege.

If Terry is successful in this action, he would be able to recover nominal as well as actual damages. If the court finds that Angela's conduct was outrageous, Terry would also be entitled to punitive damages.

QUESTION 15

Penny, a precocious 14-year-old and a devoted ice skater, left her house one Wednesday evening to go to the Ice Palace, a skating rink owned and operated by Sidney. Penny, who was alone, arrived at the rink at 8:30 p.m. and purchased a ticket. She presented the ticket to Leon, an adult, who was Sidney's regular ticket taker. Leon told Penny she must be at least 16 to enter and skate. Penny immediately declared that she was 16 and smiled so appealingly that Leon admitted her. Leon did not ask Penny for identification to verify her age although Sidney had ordered him to do so in all questionable cases. Leon later admitted that, though he suspected Penny was under age, he had often seen her around the rink and thought that if he were "nice to her," she might date him sometime.

A state statute prohibited children under the age of 16 from being in a pool hall, bowling alley, or skating rink after 7:00 p.m. unless accompanied by an adult. An operator allowing a child to be in his establishment in violation of the statute was guilty of a misdemeanor.

At about 9:30 p.m., Penny was severely injured by another skater who lost his balance when a steel blade on one of his new skates broke in half because of a crack in the blade. His skates, which bore a "Dura Skate" trademark, had been purchased from Sidney fifteen minutes before the accident occurred. In the package with the skates was a printed document containing the following provision: "In lieu of all other warranties, these skates to be free of all defects of workmanship or materials for a period of 90 days after purchase."

1. What are Penny's rights, if any, against Sidney? Discuss.

2. What are Penny's rights, if any, against Dura Company?
    Discuss.

ISSUE/FACT LADDER

Issue	Facts
Paragraph 1 Respondeat Superior / Vicarious Liability	Although Leon had been instructed by his employer to verify ages in questionable cases, he permitted 14-year-old Penny to enter the skating rink at 8:30 p.m. without verifying her age, despite his suspicion that she was underage.
Paragraph 1 Contributory Negligence	Penny lied to Leon about her age in order to enter the skating rink.
Paragraph 2 Negligence Per Se	A state statute prohibited children under 16 from entering a skating rink after 7:00 p.m. unless accompanied by an adult. Under the statute, Sidney, the owner of the skating rink, was guilty of a misdemeanor.
Paragraph 3 Causation / Damages	Penny was severely injured when struck by another skater.
Paragraph 3 Manufacturing Defect	The skater who struck Penny had lost his balance when the steel blade on one of his new skates broke in half because of a crack in the blade. The blade was manufactured by Dura Company and sold to the skater by Sidney.
Paragraph 3 Express Warranty	The package with the skates contained a warranty that the skates would be free from defects for 90 days after purchase.

OUTLINE OF ISSUES

1. What are Penny's rights, if any, against Sidney? Discuss.
2. What are Penny's rights, if any, against Dura Company? Discuss.

I. Penny v. Sidney

   A. Negligence Per Se

   B. Negligence

      1. Duty

      2. Breach of Duty

      3. Causation

      4. Damages

   C. Respondeat Superior / Vicarious Liability

   D. Express Warranty

II. Penny v. Dura Company

   A. Strict Products Liability / Manufacturing Defect

   B. Express Warranty

SUBSTANTIVE ANSWER

I. Penny v. Sidney

Penny may attempt to recover under theories of negligence per se, respondeat superior and implied warranty of merchantability.

While juries and courts usually decide what constitutes negligence, the state may also set the appropriate standard through statutes. If a statute has sufficiently close application to the facts of the case, a violation of the statute is "negligence per se." A statute is applicable to prove liability if the plaintiff is part of the *class* of persons the statute is designed to protect, the *harm* suffered is the type of harm intended to be prevented and the *standard of conduct* is clearly defined.

The statute in this case prevents children under 16 years of age from being in a skating rink after 7:00 p.m. unless accompanied by an adult. Since children may be in the rink unaccompanied by an adult earlier in the day, it is likely that the statute is meant to keep young teenagers from congregating in large numbers and idling away their evenings. The harm prevented by the statute has nothing to do with skating accidents like the one Penny suffered. The statute is not applicable to prove liability in this case because it does not meet the requirement that the harm suffered is the type of harm intended to be prevented. Sidney, the owner of the rink, is not liable for negligence under the statute.

While Sidney is not liable under the statute, Penny should raise a general negligence claim. Sidney has a duty to exercise ordinary care in keeping his property safe. It may be argued that he breached that duty by not checking everyone's equipment before entry into the rink. However, it is unlikely a court will find such a duty to inspect, or that he breached his duty to maintain a safe rink.

Sidney will not be vicariously liable under respondeat superior for any possible negligence on Leon's part for letting Penny into the rink without verifying her age. Leon did not act with the purpose of advancing Sidney's business interests but instead acted for his own interest in obtaining a date with Penny.

Penny may, however, recover under the theory of implied warranty of merchantability since Sidney sold the cracked skate which caused the other skater to strike her. All products that are packaged in labelled containers and sold regularly by businessmen are assumed to be fit for the ordinary purpose for which they are intended. This particular skate did not perform properly, causing the accident in which Penny was injured. There is no requirement for privity between the seller and the party injured.

Penny is entitled to recover medical expenses, pain and suffering and possibly mental distress. Sidney cannot claim Penny was contributorily negligent for being in the skating rink while unaccompanied by an adult. Contributory negligence is only a defense to an implied warranty claim in limited situations such as abnormal misuse of the product.

II. Penny v. Dura Company

A manufacturer is strictly liable if it places a defective product in the market that causes injury to others. A product which is normally safe may be considered defective for purposes of strict liability if it is defectively constructed due to any error or mistake; this is called a manufacturing defect. The cracked skate sold by Dura Company had a manufacturing defect because its blade was improperly constructed. Dura Company regularly engaged in the business of selling this product and the evidence suggests the product reached the consumer without any substantial change in the condition in which it was sold. The defective skate was the proximate cause of the accident which caused Penny to be injured as there were no intervening causes between the skater's accident and Penny's injury.

Since the accident occurred only fifteen minutes after the skates were purchased, it was well within the 90 day warranty period. Dura Company is liable under its express warranty because the warranty represents the skates as free of defects, which they were not. As with strict products liability, there is no requirement of privity.

Contributory negligence does not apply to Penny's conduct because she had nothing to do with the use of the product. She did not misuse the product nor was she aware of the defect. Penny may recover damages against the manufacturer for her injuries, pain and suffering and possibly mental distress.

QUESTION 16

Mrs. Park, troubled by an irritating skin rash, consulted Dr. Howe for treatment. Dr. Howe diagnosed the rash as an unusual strain of herpes transmitted by sexual contact. Mrs. Park expressed doubt about the diagnosis, indicating that she had only had sexual contact with her husband. Dr. Howe stated that he was certain of the diagnosis, and that this strain of herpes had just been introduced into the area through prostitutes who had recently arrived from another country.

Mrs. Park, upset by the diagnosis and the statements by Dr. Howe, confronted her husband with the information and accused him of infidelity. Mr. Park denied any wrongdoing and, after several days of strained communications and marital relations, persuaded his wife to obtain a second opinion.

Mrs. Park consulted the second doctor ten days after seeing Dr. Howe. The second doctor diagnosed her skin rash as a common bacterial infection and prescribed a successful treatment.

1. What are Mrs. Park's rights, if any, against Dr. Howe? Discuss.

2. What are Mr. Park's rights, if any, against Dr. Howe? Discuss.

ISSUE/FACT LADDER

Issue	Facts
Paragraph 1 Negligence	Dr. Howe misdiagnosed Mrs. Park's common bacterial infection as an unusual strain of herpes.
Paragraph 1 Negligence	Dr. Howe stated he was certain of the diagnosis after Mrs. Park expressed doubt and indicated that she had only had sexual contact with her husband.
Paragraph 1 Slander Per Se	Dr. Howe implied that Mr. Park had contracted herpes form prostitutes who had recently arrived from another country.
Paragraph 2 Negligent Infliction of Emotional Distress	Mrs. Park, upset by the diagnosis and Dr. Howe's statements, confronted her husband and accused him of infidelity.
Paragraph 2 Loss of Consortium	The Parks had several days of strained communications and marital relations.

OUTLINE OF ISSUES

1. What are Mrs. Park's rights, if any, against Dr. Howe? Discuss.
2. What are Mr. Park's rights, if any, against Dr. Howe? Discuss.

I. Mrs. Park v. Dr. Howe

    A.   Negligence

        1. Duty

        2. Breach

        3. Causation

        4. Damages

II. Mr. Park v. Dr. Howe

    A. Defamation

        1. Slander Per Se

        2. Qualified Privilege — Doctor-Patient Relationship

    B. Interference with Family Relations — Alienation of Affections

    C. Negligent Infliction of Emotional Distress

SUBSTANTIVE ANSWER

I. Mrs. Park v. Dr. Howe

Mrs. Park will probably bring a negligence suit against Dr. Howe.

A physician has the duty to act with reasonable care to avoid the unreasonable risk of harm to a patient. Whether a physician has used reasonable care is often determined by local community standards. However, many courts have replaced local community standards with national standards, since physicians are nationally certified. Whether a local or a national standard is applied, it is likely that Dr. Howe did not use reasonable care in diagnosing Mrs. Park's rash, as the rash he misdiagnosed as an unusual virus was classified as common by another local physician. Further, Mrs. Park may be able to use expert testimony to prove that a reasonable physician would have rechecked her rash after she indicated that her relationship with her husband was monogamous.

Mrs. Park should recover for all damages which proximately resulted from Dr. Howe's negligence. His misdiagnosis and his statements concerning her husband caused Mrs. Park to be upset. Dr. Howe may assert that her distress was not proximately caused by his misdiagnosis, but rather from the subsequent strained relationship with her husband which was caused by her accusation of infidelity. However, Mrs. Park's actions would not be a superseding intervening cause, given the foreseeability of such an accusation by a person in a monogamous relationship diagnosed with a sexually transmitted disease. Thus, Dr. Howe's negligent misdiagnosis may be deemed the proximate cause of all Mrs. Park's emotional distress, including that arising from her strained relationship with her husband.

One may only recover actual damages in a negligence action. Dr. Howe may question the genuineness of her distress since it was unaccompanied by any physical injuries. Those courts which require a showing of physical injury to prove emotional distress have often been willing to make exceptions in extreme cases such as the mishandling of a corpse or the negligent transmission of a telegram, where the acts by nature would give rise to emotional distress. These courts might consider the assertion that one has a contagious sexually transmitted disease, accompanied by an insinuation that one's exclusive sexual partner contracted the disease from a prostitute, extreme enough to assume that genuine emotional distress was suffered. Further, some courts have abandoned the requirement that physical injuries be shown and have left it to the jury to decide if a reasonable person would have suffered genuine emotional distress under the circumstances.

Mrs. Park may also recover for the loss of consortium if she can prove that Mr. Park withheld sexual relations after she accused him of infidelity.

II. Mr. Park v. Dr. Howe

Mr. Park could sue Dr. Howe for defamation for implying to Mrs. Park that he had contracted herpes from prostitutes who had recently arrived from another country. Mr. Park would have to prove that Dr. Howe intentionally or negligently published a defamatory statement which caused actual damages.

Although the implication would probably be considered a medical opinion, usually not defamatory, it is likely Dr. Howe's misdiagnosis will be actionable as defamation. An opinion may give rise to liability when it implies undisclosed facts which would be defamatory if published. Dr. Howe's medical opinion was that Mrs. Park had herpes, which given the surrounding circumstances led to the implication that Mr. Park contracted herpes from prostitutes. This implication would be considered slander if spoken, and could reasonably be interpreted by a jury as being defamatory.

Publication occurs when a defamatory statement is conveyed and understood by at least one other person. The publication in this case occurred when Dr. Howe implied that Mr. Park had contracted herpes from prostitutes. This statement was communicated to Mrs. Park after her examination, and since she subsequently went home and accused her husband of infidelity, presumably she understood the implications of the statements by Dr. Howe.

In a defamation action, the plaintiff must also prove that the defendant had the intent to publish, not necessarily to defame. In this case, Dr. Howe negligently implied to Mrs. Park that her husband had contracted herpes from prostitutes when he negligently misdiagnosed a common rash. In addition, he failed to recheck her rash after she told him that she was monogamous. These actions led to the negligent publication of the defamatory statement, making it likely that Mr. Park would win in an action for slander.

Dr. Howe may, because of the doctor-patient relationship, argue that he had a qualified privilege to make these statements as part of a diagnosis he believed to be correct. However, this privilege does not normally extend to defamatory statements. Even if such a privilege was justified, it probably would not extend here since his misdiagnosis involved gross negligence. A doctor who exercised reasonable care would, under the circumstances, have rechecked the rash before making such defamatory implications.

A plaintiff who has been slandered must normally prove special damages, i.e., the plaintiff must prove some specific pecuniary loss. However, in this case Dr. Howe implied that Mr. Park had a "loathsome disease." This is an exception to the general damages rule for slander. Dr. Howe's implication is considered slander per se and all damages are presumed. Therefore, Mr. Park may recover damages for any emotional distress that he suffered as a result of Dr. Howe's defamatory statements.

Mr. Park may also sue Dr. Howe for the negligent infliction of emotional distress, using the same arguments as Mrs. Park. His recovery will depend on whether the court requires a showing of a physical injury to prove the emotional distress. Mr. Park may also recover for the loss of consortium if he can prove that Mrs. Park withheld sexual relations after she accused him of infidelity.

QUESTION 17

The four-story law school building of Blond University, a private institution open to the public, had a defective elevator which frequently stopped between floors. The elevator had an alarm button which, when pressed, would ring a bell in the hallway to alert persons in the building to the fact that the elevator had stopped between floors with passengers inside it. The defective condition did not create any danger that the elevator might fall or otherwise physically injure any passenger.

Elco, an elevator maintenance company, had a contract with Blond University to inspect, service and maintain the elevator.

One night, Michele, a law teacher, and her secretary, Paul, were working late on an overdue manuscript in Michele's office on the fourth floor of the building. They entered the elevator about 11:20 p.m. to go home. Although the official closing hour for the building was 11:00 p.m., there were exit doors from the building which could be opened from the inside. Both Michele and Paul knew that the elevator frequently stopped between floors.

The elevator stopped between the second and third floors. Michele pressed the alarm button and the bell rang in the hallway. Julian, a law student, was the only other person still in the building. He heard the alarm bell and realized that someone was trapped in the elevator. He thought this was very funny and he deliberately did not call the campus maintenance staff. Michele and Paul were not discovered and released until 8 a.m. the next day.

Michele suffered from high blood pressure. This condition and her fright at being confined in the elevator caused her to sustain a heart attack after two hours in the elevator.

Paul suffered severe emotional distress due to being confined in the elevator and his fear that Michele was dying. Furthermore, he was subsequently embarrassed and humiliated by the remarks of students who suggested that perhaps some amorous activity in the elevator might have caused Michele's heart attack.

1. What are Michele and Paul's rights, if any, against Julian?
   Discuss.

2. What are Michele and Paul's rights, if any, against Elco?
   Discuss.

3. What are Michele and Paul's rights, if any, against Blond
   University? Discuss.

ISSUE/FACT LADDER

Issue	Facts
Paragraph 1 Negligence	Blond University had a defective elevator which frequently stopped between floors.
Paragraph 2 Independent Contractor / Nondelegable Duty	Elco, an elevator maintenance company, had a contract with Blond University to inspect, service and maintain the elevator.
Paragraph 3 Scope of Employment	Michele, a law teacher, and her secretary, Paul, were working late on an overdue manuscript in Michele's office on the fourth floor of the building.
Paragraph 3 Comparative Negligence / Contributory Negligence	Both Michele and Paul knew when they entered the elevator that it frequently stopped between floors.
Paragraph 4 Affirmative Duty	Julian, a law student, was the only other person in the building when he heard the alarm bell and realized that someone was trapped in the elevator.
Paragraph 5 Damages	Michele suffered a heart attack after two hours in the elevator.
Paragraph 6 Damages / Negligent Infliction of Emotional Distress	Paul suffered severe emotional distress from being confined in the elevator and his fear that Michele was dying.

OUTLINE OF ISSUES

1. What are Michele and Paul's rights, if any, against Julian? Discuss.
2. What are Michele and Paul's rights, if any, against Elco? Discuss.
3. What are Michele and Paul's rights, if any, against Blond University? Discuss.

I. Michele and Paul v. Julian

   A. Infliction of Emotional Distress

   B. Affirmative Duty

II. Michele and Paul v. Elco

   A. Negligence

      1. Duty and Breach

      2. Causation

      3. Damages

   B. Comparative Negligence / Contributory Negligence

III.   Michele and Paul v. Blond University

   A. Negligence

      1. Duty and Breach

      2. Causation

      3. Damages

   B. Comparative Negligence / Contributory Negligence

   C. Vicarious Liability / Nondelegable Duty

   D. Worker's Compensation

SUBSTANTIVE ANSWER

Michele's and Paul's possible tort actions will be discussed together since they both could bring the same actions using the same analysis. The only difference will be in the discussion of possible damages that they could receive.

I. Michele and Paul v. Julian

Michele and Paul could bring actions against Julian for the intentional infliction of emotional distress. This tort occurs when one intentionally or recklessly causes severe emotional damage to another through extreme and outrageous conduct. However, a failure to act will not be considered intentional or reckless unless the person had a duty to act.

Julian failed to notify school officials that the elevator was stuck. However, he had no affirmative duty to rescue Michele and Paul from the stranded elevator. Generally, a person does not have a duty to act for the benefit of another. The exceptions to this rule involve situations where there is a special relationship, where one assumes a duty, or where one creates the risk. Julian, as a law student, had no special relationship with either Michele or Paul. He did not assume a duty of care because he took no action at all. Finally, he did not create the risk through his inaction; Michele and Paul would have been trapped in the elevator regardless of Julian's actions. Therefore, Julian owed no duty of care to Michele and Paul and is not liable for the intentional infliction of emotional distress.

Furthermore, under this analysis Michele and Paul would be unable to bring actions against Julian for negligence or the negligent infliction of emotional distress.

II. Michele and Paul v. Elco

Michele and Paul could bring actions against Elco under the theory of negligence. They would have to prove that Elco had a duty, which it breached, causing damages.

Elco, an elevator maintenance company, had a contract with Blond University to inspect, service, and maintain the elevator. Therefore, Elco had a duty to exercise reasonable care that the elevator they serviced was safe and in good working condition. Michele and Paul could argue that since the elevator frequently got stuck between floors, Elco breached its duty to inspect, service, and maintain the elevator. Whether this condition was caused by their inaction in fixing the elevator, or by their misfeasance when fixing the elevator, Elco has breached its duty of care to the users of the elevator.

Elco's breach was the actual cause of the injuries to Michele and Paul. "But for" Elco's negligence, Michele and Paul would not have been stuck in the elevator and would not have been injured. Elco's negligence was also the proximate cause of their injuries. It was foreseeable that a person who got stuck in the elevator might suffer emotional distress from the incident. The fact that Julian failed to help was not a superseding cause, since it was quite possible that no one would have come to their aid until the following morning.

Elco will probably argue that Michele and Paul were negligent in getting into an elevator which they knew frequently stopped between floors because it was late at night and the building was closed. Thus, they assumed the risk that if the elevator became stuck, as it frequently did, they might have to remain in the elevator until someone could let them out in the morning. If the court finds that Michele and Paul assumed the risk of being stuck in the elevator, and recognizes the doctrine of contributory negligence, they will be barred from recovery. However, if the court recognizes the doctrine of comparative negligence, the court will divide the liability between Michele and Paul and Elco based on their relative degrees of fault.

Michele will be able to recover damages for her medical bills, as well as damages for pain and suffering and lost income. The mere fact that she had high blood pressure will not make her an extra-sensitive plaintiff. Paul might be able to recover for his severe emotional distress. However, if he cannot show physical symptoms of the stress, he will only recover if the court finds this to be an extreme case. For example, the mishandling of a corpse is often considered an extreme case. Paul will not be able to recover for his damaged reputation since it was not foreseeable to Elco that his being stuck in the elevator would lead to damaging rumors.

III. Michele and Paul v. Blond University

Michele and Paul could bring actions against Blond University under the theory of negligence. They would have to prove that Blond University had a duty, which it breached, causing damages. They may also try to recover for their injuries under worker's compensation.

Blond University has a duty to hire qualified, nonnegligent workers. Michele and Paul may argue that Blond University breached this duty when it failed to fire Elco despite the fact that the elevator was frequently stuck between floors. Blond University's knowledge of this condition indicates that it was aware of Elco's negligence in maintaining the elevator. By failing to remedy this situation, they breached their duty of care. The injuries which resulted were foreseeable to Blond University; therefore, it was both the actual and proximate cause of Michele and Paul's injuries. Elco's negligence would not be a superseding cause since it was known to Blond University and, thus, completely foreseeable.

Blond University will probably make the same argument as Elco, claiming that Michele and Paul were negligent when they entered an elevator which they knew frequently got stuck between floors and, therefore, should be barred from recovery. As stated earlier, their ability to recover damages will be determined by whether the court recognizes the doctrine of contributory negligence or comparative negligence. The damages Michele and Paul would be able to receive would also be the same as they could receive against Elco.

Even if Blond University was not negligent in hiring Elco, it still may be liable for any negligence by Elco. Usually employers are not held vicariously liable for the negligence of independent contractors because these workers are not subject to the control of the employer. Although Elco was an independent contractor, Blond University may still be liable if the court determines the duty to maintain a safe, working elevator is nondelegable. Public policy generally makes certain duties nondelegable. Blond University's liability will depend on how important the court deems the duty of maintaining a safe, working elevator. Since the school is open to the public, the court may equate Blond University's duty of care to that of a city in maintaining its public streets. In this instance, Blond University would be liable for the same damages as Elco.

Michele and Paul could also try to recover under worker's compensation. Even if they were found to be negligent, they could obtain a limited contribution from Blond University in an amount proportional to the employer's percentage of negligence. Blond University may argue that the building was closed and, therefore, their injuries were not sustained during the course of their employment. However, considering that they were working late on an overdue manuscript in Michele's office, it is likely that the court will find this activity beneficial to their employer and within the scope of their employment. Thus, Blond University will be at least partially responsible for compensating their injuries.

QUESTION 18

Twenty years ago Resco erected a building in what was then an unsettled area. Resco conducts experimental work in connection with cattle virus diseases in that building. The area surrounding the Resco property has now become a thriving cattle and dairy district.

Cattle ranchers in the area tried to induce Zoe, a cattle auctioneer, to establish a local market. Zoe was reluctant to do so because of his fear that a virus might escape from Resco's property and infect cattle.

Some of the ranchers called on Bill, the president of Resco. They told Bill of their desire to establish a market in the area and asked him to make a statement which would dispel Zoe's fears.

Bill called a conference and, without having made any investigation and without naming Zoe, stated that there was "no danger at all" of any virus escaping from the Resco premises, and that only a "driveling idiot" could conclude otherwise. This statement was printed in "News," a local newspaper, and received wide attention. As a result, Zoe was frequently referred to in the community as the "driveling idiot." This caused him considerable embarrassment.

In the belief that Bill's statement concerning the safety of the Resco operation was correct and in order to escape further embarrassment, Zoe established a market in the area for the auction of cattle. Shortly thereafter, without negligence on the part of Resco, a virus escaped from Resco's premises and infected cattle in the area.

To stop the spread of the infection, public authorities ordered the slaughter of all infected or exposed cattle and Zoe had to abandon his market with consequent financial loss to him.

1. What are Zoe's rights, if any, against Resco? Discuss.

2. What are Zoe's rights, if any, against Bill? Discuss.

3. What are Zoe's rights, if any, against "News"? Discuss.

ISSUE/FACT LADDER

Issue	Facts
Paragraph 1 Ultrahazardous Activity	Twenty years ago, Resco constructed a building to conduct experimental work in connection with cattle virus diseases.
Paragraph 1 Coming to the Nuisance	Once an unsettled region, the area surrounding the building became a thriving cattle district.
Paragraph 4 Negligent Misrepresentation / Vicarious Liability	Bill, the president of Resco, stated publicly that there was "no danger at all" of any virus escaping and that only a "driveling idiot" would think otherwise. He made this statement for the purpose of inducing Zoe, a cattle auctioneer, to establish a local market. Zoe had been reluctant to do so because of his fear that a virus might escape from Resco's building and infect cattle. Bill had not made any investigation about this possibility before making his statement.
Paragraph 4 Defamation	Bill's statement was printed in the "News." While Bill did not refer to Zoe by name, Zoe was frequently referred to in the community as a "driveling idiot" as a result of the article.
Paragraph 5 Misrepresentation / Negligent Misrepresentation	In reliance on Bill's statement that Resco's building was safe and to escape further embarrassment in the community, Zoe established an auction market.
Paragraph 5 Ultrahazardous Activity / Nuisance	Shortly thereafter, without negligence on Resco's part, a virus escaped from Resco's premises and infected local cattle.

Paragraph 6 Causation / Damages	Public authorities were forced to order the slaughter of all infected or exposed cattle. Zoe had to abandon his market and suffered consequent financial loss.

OUTLINE OF ISSUES

1. What are Zoe's rights, if any, against Resco? Discuss.
2. What are Zoe's rights, if any, against Bill? Discuss.
3 What are Zoe's rights, if any, against "News"? Discuss.

I. Zoe v. Resco

   A. Ultrahazardous Activity

   B. Nuisance

   C. Vicarious Liability / Respondeat Superior

II. Zoe v. Bill

   A. Misrepresentation / Negligent Misrepresentation

   B. Defamation

III.   Zoe v. "News"

SUBSTANTIVE ANSWER

I. Zoe v. Resco

Zoe should claim that Resco is strictly liable because experimental work with cattle virus diseases is an ultrahazardous activity. Some factors the court will look at include the degree of risk of harm to property, the seriousness of the harm that could result, whether the activity can be performed safely, whether the activity is commonly engaged in, the value of the activity and the location at which it is performed. The court is likely to hold that Resco is strictly liable because it appears these experiments cannot be carried out safely, even with reasonable care. Resco was not negligent and yet the accident still occurred. In addition, Zoe was not an abnormally sensitive plaintiff, nor an unforeseeable one, and he was damaged by the kind of risk that made the activity ultrahazardous to begin with.

Resco cannot claim contributory negligence because Zoe did not knowingly, voluntarily and unreasonably subject himself to the danger of the virus. He only established the market after he was assured there was no risk of this type of accident.

While Zoe most likely will recover under ultrahazardous activity, he should also raise a nuisance claim if he wants to obtain an injunction barring Resco from conducting further virus experiments. In order to win under nuisance, Zoe must show that his use and enjoyment of his property was interfered with in a substantial way and that Resco's activities were abnormally dangerous. Resco should claim that Zoe assumed the risk by "coming to the nuisance." Zoe knew Resco had been operating in the area for a long time before he opened his market there. However, modern courts do not usually treat this as an absolute defense. The court is more likely to hold that "coming to the nuisance" is a defense only if the defendant's activity is appropriate in the area where it occurred, and the plaintiff's own activity was inappropriate for the area. Establishing a cattle market in a thriving cattle and dairy district seems appropriate whereas experimenting with deadly cattle viruses in the same area seems like a recipe for disaster.

Resco will only be vicariously liable under respondeat superior for any of the torts Bill may have committed if Bill acted with the purpose of advancing Resco's business. The facts suggest that Bill was acting within his capacity as president of Resco when he made his statement about the safety of Resco's operations. Therefore, Resco is likely to be held vicariously liable.

Zoe will recover for any property damage such as lost cattle he may have purchased. He will also recover for present and future earnings.

II. Zoe v. Bill

Zoe should claim that Bill is liable under the tort of intentional misrepresentation for his statement that there was "no danger at all" of a virus escaping. For Zoe to recover under this tort, he must show there was a misrepresentation, a culpable state of mind, an intent to induce reliance, justifiable reliance and damages. Clearly there was a misrepresentation because a virus did escape after Bill asserted that there was "no danger at all." However, Zoe will have trouble showing that Bill had the culpable state of mind, or scienter. He must show that Bill knew or believed he was not telling the truth, or did not have any confidence in his statement but stated or implied that he did, or knew that he did not have grounds for his statement but stated or implied he did. Whether Bill's statements meet any of these criteria is a factual question but it is important to note that the main function of the scienter requirement is to prevent merely negligent misrepresentations from being actionable. Because the court may end its analysis of intentional misrepresentation at this point, the inducement and justifiable reliance requirements will be discussed below under negligent misrepresentation.

If Zoe cannot establish scienter, he should still claim negligent misrepresentation which courts have recently begun to recognize. This would allow Zoe to recover for a misrepresentation which was merely negligent, rather than intentional. Except for scienter requirement, the standards for measuring this tort are the same as for intentional misrepresentation.

Zoe would likely recover under the theory of negligent misrepresentation. Bill was at least negligent because he breached his duty of care by making his bold statement without conducting any investigation as to whether it was actually true. While Bill did not mention any names in his statement, the facts suggest that it was made to induce Zoe to open a market. As Bill was the president of Resco, a court would probably view Zoe as justifiably relying on Bill's statement assuring the safety of the facility. Zoe suffered damages when all the infected cattle were slaughtered and he had to abandon his market. As mentioned above, Resco probably will be held vicariously liable for this.

Courts have applied two different measures of damages for misrepresentations. The "reliance" measure, as with contract law, attempts to put the plaintiff in the position he was in before the misrepresentation. The "expectation" measure attempts to put the plaintiff in the position he would have been in had the misrepresented information been true. The court would apply the reliance measure here because the expectation damages are only used when there is a contract between the plaintiff and defendant. Zoe would also recover for any consequential damages.

For a plaintiff to recover under defamation, the defendant must have made a false and defamatory statement which was communicated to a person other than the plaintiff. There also must be fault amounting to at least negligence on the part of the defendant, and a special harm to the plaintiff. Defamation protects against a tendency to harm the reputation of the plaintiff but it does not apply to a pure expression of an opinion. The "driveling idiot" statement merely expresses Bill's opinion, and does not imply any real claim about Zoe's or anybody else's mental capacity. Zoe will not recover under defamation against Bill.

Zoe v. "News"

As mentioned above, Zoe cannot recover under defamation. "News" merely printed a pure expressions of opinion which is not actionable. Zoe does not have any other claims against "News."

QUESTION 19

Rob, the manager of J & M's department store, adopted a policy of stopping people at random as they were leaving the store and asking them whether they had taken certain items which were usually shoplifted. Katie, a housewife, was stopped and questioned in this manner and when she appeared to be flustered, Rob told her to go back to his office. When she hesitated, he placed his hand on her shoulder and turned her in that direction. Katie then proceeded to the office without any further assistance from him. When they reached the office, Rob told her to sit down and wait until he returned with the police.

Instead of going for the police, Rob closed, but did not lock, the office door and stepped into an adjoining office where he photographed Katie through a one-way mirror to see if she would try to hide anything she might be carrying on her person. Katie could not see him and after a few moments went to the mirror to fix her makeup. As she passed in front of a floor fan her skirt was blown up, revealing her underwear.

When Rob saw that Katie was not trying to hide anything, he returned to the office and said that he had decided not to call the police. Rob apologized for having detained her, saying that with so many items being shoplifted he couldn't be too careful, then escorted her to the door.

Katie was severely distressed about the entire incident and brought a tort action after a friend who worked at J & M's told her about the one-way mirror in Rob's office. J & M then attempted to prosecute her for shoplifting, hoping it would induce her to drop her civil action. Although there was an eyewitness who said Katie was acting suspiciously, the charges were dismissed for lack of evidence.

What are Katie's rights, if any, against J & M? Discuss.

ISSUE/FACT LADDER

Issue	Facts
Paragraph 1 Vicarious Liability	Rob, the manager of J & M's department store, adopted a policy of stopping people at random as they were leaving the store and asking them whether they had taken certain items.
Paragraph 1 False Imprisonment	Katie was stopped and questioned about shoplifting and when she appeared to be flustered, Rob told her to go back to his office. When she hesitated, he placed his hand on her shoulder and turned her in that direction. When they reached the office, Rob told her to sit down and wait until he returned with the police.
Paragraph 1 Battery	Rob placed his hand on her shoulder and turned her in the direction of his office.
Paragraph 2 False Imprisonment	Instead of going for the police, Rob closed, but did not lock, the office door and stepped into an adjoining office.
Paragraph 2 Invasion of Privacy	Rob watched Katie through a one-way mirror. Katie could not see him and after a few moments went to the mirror, fixed her makeup, unbuttoned her blouse to adjust her bra, and returned to the chair.
Paragraph 4 Damages	Katie was severely distressed about the entire incident.
Paragraph 4 Misuse of Legal Procedure	J & M attempted to prosecute her for shoplifting, hoping it would induce her to drop her civil action, but the charges were dismissed due to a lack of evidence.

OUTLINE OF ISSUES

What are Katie's rights, if any, against J & M? Discuss.

I. Vicarious Liability

II. Intentional Torts

   A. Battery

      1. Harmful or Offensive Contact

      2. Intent to Make Contact

   B. False Imprisonment

      1. Elements

      2. Shopkeeper's Privilege

III.   Invasion of Privacy and Defamation

   A. Intrusion Upon Seclusion

   B. False Light

   C. Defamation

IV.   Misuse of Legal Procedure

   A. Malicious Prosecution

   B. Abuse of Process

V. Intentional Infliction of Emotional Distress

   A. Intent

   B. Severe Emotional Damage

   C. Extreme and Outrageous Conduct

SUBSTANTIVE ANSWER

I. Vicarious Liability

An employer is liable for the torts an employee commits while acting within the scope of employment. All actions by employees that are closely connected to the employee's work which are done to advance the employer's business interest are considered to be within the employee's scope of employment. Rob's conduct, as the manager of the department store, was clearly in advance of J & M's business interest to deter shoplifting. Rob's conduct was not to advance any personal interests and, therefore, would fall within the scope of his employment.

An employer is also liable for intentional torts committed by an employee if they were done for the benefit of the employer's business. However, some courts allow liability only if the tort was reasonably foreseeable by the employer. It should be foreseeable to J & M that in attempting to deter shoplifting, its employees may take careless actions which could possibly lead to battery or false imprisonment. Therefore, J & M will be vicariously liable for all of the torts discussed in this question that were committed by Rob.

II. Intentional Torts

Katie could sue J & M for the intentional torts of battery and false imprisonment.

Katie has a right to be free from harmful or offensive contact. This right is protected under the tort of battery. To succeed in this action, Katie would have to prove that there was an intentional harmful or offensive touching by Rob to her person. It appears that Rob had the necessary intent to make contact when he placed his hand on her shoulder and turned her in the direction of his office. However, this contact was not harmful to her and it is questionable whether it would seem offensive to the reasonable person. Rob had suspected Katie of shoplifting. When he told her to go to his office, she hesitated. The jury must decide whether Rob's touching of Katie was appropriate under the given circumstances.

Katie has a right to be free from intentional restraint to a confined area. This right is protected under the tort of false imprisonment. Restraint can be accomplished by physical barriers, force, or threats against a person, property, or a third person. Since Katie was left alone in Rob's unlocked office, a jury may find there was not sufficient restraint. It is also questionable whether Katie failed to utilize a reasonable means of escape since she simply could have walked out of his office. J & M will argue that Katie impliedly consented to the confinement when she failed to object to being placed in the office, and remained once she was there. In addition, several courts have allowed a storekeeper the privilege to temporarily detain for investigation a person who is reasonably suspected of shoplifting. Under this doctrine, J & M's liability will depend on whether the court determines that the policy of stopping people at random, and detaining them when they seemed flustered, was reasonable.

If Katie is successful in either of these intentional tort actions, she will be able to recover actual and nominal damages, as well as punitive damages, if Rob's conduct was outrageous.

III. Invasion of Privacy and Defamation

Katie could also bring an action against J & M for invasion of privacy, under the theories of intrusion upon seclusion and false light, as well as an action for defamation.

Katie has a right to be free from intrusion upon the solitude and seclusion of her private life and affairs. This intrusion must be into a private place to be actionable. Katie could argue that Rob intruded upon her privacy by photographing her through the one-way mirror. It is questionable whether she would be able to recover for this since the intrusion occurred in Rob's office, which was not a private place to Katie. However, since Rob's photographing of Katie included an intrusion into a private portion of her person, i.e., when he saw her underwear as the fan blew up her skirt, this intrusion would be actionable. It was an invasion into a private portion of her body that would be highly offensive to a reasonable person.

Katie has a right to be free from publicity which places her in a false light. She can argue that by bringing charges against her for shoplifting, J & M has created the perception that she is a criminal. While this would be highly offensive to a reasonable person, the action may fail since it is doubtful that Katie was actually placed in the public eye. The charges against her would only be known to a limited group of people, not the general public.

Katie could also bring an action for defamation. She would have to prove that J & M intentionally published a defamatory statement about her to a third party. She could argue that when J & M intentionally brought shoplifting charges against her, it published a defamatory statement, to the police, that detracted from her reputation. Since these charges implied that she was a criminal, this defamation is slander per se and all damages will be presumed. Katie may also recover punitive damages if she can prove that J & M acted with malice when making the defamatory statements.

IV. Misuse of Legal Procedure

Katie could also bring actions against J & M for malicious prosecution and abuse of process.

To bring a successful action for malicious prosecution, Katie must prove that there was a criminal proceeding maliciously brought against her by J & M that lacked probable cause and which was terminated in her favor. J & M brought charges against Katie for shoplifting that were later dropped because of a lack of evidence. She, therefore, must prove that there was no probable cause and that J & M acted with malice. If Katie can prove that J & M's sole purpose in bringing the charges was to induce her to drop her civil action, she will be able to show malice. It is questionable whether an eyewitness who said Katie was acting suspiciously is enough to warrant probable cause. If the action succeeds, Katie would be able to recover for actual harm to her reputation, emotional distress and lost income, as well as punitive damages.

If the action for malicious prosecution fails, Katie could also bring an action for abuse of process. This tort action allows a person to recover when a valid cause of action is brought for the wrong reasons. Even if the court determines there was probable cause in bringing the charges, she may recover if she could prove that J & M's sole purpose in bringing the charges was to induce her to drop her civil action.

V. Intentional Infliction of Emotional Distress

Finally, Katie could bring an action against J & M for the intentional infliction of emotional distress. This occurs when one intentionally or recklessly causes severe emotional damage to another through extreme and outrageous conduct.

If Katie succeeds in her action for malicious prosecution, it is likely she will be able to prove that J & M's false shoplifting charge constituted extreme and outrageous conduct which recklessly disregarded the high probability that emotional distress would occur. However, if the action for malicious prosecution is defeated because probable cause existed, it is unlikely that J & M's conduct will be considered extreme or outrageous.

Katie may also have difficulty proving that she sustained injuries. The courts often hold that accompanying physical injuries are necessary to prove that the emotional distress was severe. If so, Katie will not be able to recover unless the court considers this an extreme case, such as the mishandling of a corpse, where the emotional distress is presumed. Furthermore, some courts have abandoned the requirement that physical injuries be shown and have left it to the jury to decide if a reasonable person would have suffered genuine emotional distress under the circumstances.

QUESTION 20

Twenty years ago, Ed worked in the research department of Dynorad, a private armaments manufacturer doing substantial business with the government. At the time, Ed and his colleagues were testing a newly developed strain of bacteria for use in germ warfare. From tests on animals, they found the agent to be effective, and it has since been incorporated into weapons sold to the government. The strain of bacteria has never been used in combat and has never been tested on humans. However, Ed was accidentally exposed to the bacteria because of inadequate safety mechanisms at Dynorad's laboratories.

The exposure was very brief and Ed did not suffer immediate harm, but his health has gradually deteriorated. It recently became so poor that he checked into a hospital. Doctors quickly traced his maladies to the bacteria, but cannot cure him.

Ralph, a reporter for Courier Journal, learned of Ed's condition and entered Ed's hospital room wearing a white coat and stethoscope. Ed, thinking that Ralph was a doctor, disclosed that his mental capacities were impaired, that a lung and a kidney were no longer functioning, that he wore a wig because all his hair had fallen out and that he was now impotent.

The next day Ralph published a story attacking the use of inhumane weapons by the government and the lack of safety precautions used by local arms manufacturers such as Dynorad. The story included Ed's name, an account of his accident twenty years ago and a description of the symptoms that Ed had disclosed to Ralph.

1. What are Ed's rights, if any, against Dynorad? Discuss.

2. What are Ed's rights, if any, against Courier Journal?
   Discuss.

ISSUE/FACT LADDER

Issue	Facts
Paragraph 1 Ultrahazardous Activity	Twenty years ago, Dynorad, a private armaments manufacturer, was testing strains of bacteria for use in germ warfare weaponry.
Paragraph 1 Negligence	A worker for Dynorad, Ed, was exposed to bacteria because of Dynorad's inadequate safety mechanisms.
Paragraph 2 Statute of Limitations	Ed suffered no immediate harm. However, over the twenty years since his exposure, his health gradually deteriorated and he recently had to check into the hospital. He cannot be cured.
Paragraph 3 Invasion of Privacy / Misrepresentation	Ralph, a reporter for Courier Journal, entered Ed's hospital room dressed in a white coat and stethoscope. Ed disclosed his myriad of health problems, believing Ralph was a doctor.
Paragraph 4 Invasion of Privacy / Intentional Infliction of Emotional Distress	The next day, Ralph published a story in the Courier Journal attacking the use of inhumane weapons and the lack of safety precautions used by local arms manufacturers such as Dynorad. The story included Ed's name, an account of his exposure twenty years ago and a description of the symptoms Ed had disclosed to Ralph.

OUTLINE OF ISSUES

1. What are Ed's rights, if any, against Dynorad? Discuss.
2. What are Ed's rights, if any, against Courier Journal? Discuss.

I. Ed v. Dynorad

   A. Ultrahazardous Activity

   B. Negligence

      1. Duty

      2. Breach

      3. Causation

      4. Damages

   C. Statute of Limitation

II. Ed v. Courier Journal

   A. Respondeat Superior / Vicarious Liability

   B. Invasion of Privacy

      1. Intrusion Upon Seclusion

      2. Public Disclosure of Embarrassing Private Facts

   C. Misrepresentation

   D. Intentional Infliction of Emotional Distress

      1. Intent

      2. Severe Emotional Damage

      3. Extreme and Outrageous Conduct

SUBSTANTIVE ANSWER

I. Ed v. Dynorad

Ed should claim that Dynorad is liable for his injuries because testing bacteria for germ warfare weaponry is an ultrahazardous activity. There is strict liability for activities that involve an inherent and substantial risk of harm. Some factors the court will look at include the degree of risk of harm, the seriousness of the harm that could result, whether the activity can be performed safely, whether the activity is commonly engaged in, the value of the activity and the location at which it is performed. Like nuclear reactors and storage of explosives, the court may consider germ warfare experiments to be one of those activities which is so inherently dangerous it outweighs all other factors and, thus, warrants strict liability. Worker exposure to dangerous bacteria is most likely a foreseeable risk to a foreseeable plaintiff.

Dynorad may argue that Ed assumed the risk of such accidents by accepting employment in the research department of a germ weapons manufacturer. However, this defense is only applicable if the plaintiff knowingly, voluntarily and unreasonably subjects himself to the kind of risk that makes the activity ultrahazardous. A court is not likely to hold that a worker unreasonably subjects himself to such danger by merely accepting employment. It may be reasonable for a worker to expect that an employer's safety mechanisms and procedures will insure his safety.

Ed may also pursue a negligence claim against Dynorad for its inadequate safety mechanisms. Dynorad had a duty as an employer to provide its employees with adequate safety features in the laboratory to prevent reasonably foreseeable accidents. It breached that duty because the safety mechanisms were inadequate to prevent human exposure to bacteria. The accident was the proximate cause of Ed's deteriorating health and incurable condition because it was foreseeable that without adequate safety measures, a worker could be exposed to the deadly bacteria.

Dynorad may attempt to argue that it has government immunity from negligence claims since it manufactures weaponry for the government. Its claim would be based on the idea that weapons manufacturing is a public function that is analogous to police and fire departments. This claim is sure to fail because Dynorad is a private corporation and activities which produce revenues are generally not given any immunity. In any case, it is doubtful that even the federal government would have immunity under these facts.

Dynorad may also claim the statute of limitations as a defense to negligence. Ed's exposure occurred twenty years ago and Dynorad may argue that Ed is now barred from bringing a cause of action based on that event. However, modern courts have held that the statute of limitations does not begin to run until after the injury is discovered or would have been discovered by a reasonable person. Dynorad still might argue that a reasonable person would have gone to the hospital and received diagnosis as soon as his health had begun to deteriorate instead of waiting twenty years until his health was so bad that he required hospitalization. Whether Ed acted as a reasonable person is a factual question to be decided by the jury.

II. Ed v. Courier Journal

Ed will argue that Courier Journal is vicariously liable under the doctrine of respondeat superior for the torts committed by Ralph. Ralph went to the hospital and obtained the information from Ed in order to write the article for Courier Journal. He was acting with an intent to further his employer's business purpose and Courier Journal is likely to be found liable even if Ralph's methods were unwise and even forbidden by the Journal.

Ed should claim invasion of privacy. This tort protects a plaintiff's right to be left alone, to dignity, confidentiality and the right to control how one is portrayed to the public. Ed has a claim under the theories of intrusion upon seclusion and public disclosure of embarrassing private facts.

The intrusion upon seclusion cause of action is triggered when a private place is invaded and this invasion is offensive to a reasonable person. Ralph entered Ed's hospital room in attire that gave the impression he was a doctor and proceeded to attain deeply personal information from Ed about his health problems. A court may regard a hospital room as a private place, and Ralph's methods of gathering information may be offensive to the average person. Courier Journal cannot defend by claiming a privilege under the First Amendment, since it does not extend to situations where a reporter uses false pretenses to gain access to private information. *See Dietemann v. Time., Inc.* Ed can recover for pure emotional distress and mental anguish and need not prove any special damages.

Ed also has a claim under the category of public disclosure of embarrassing private facts because Courier Journal published his name and a description of his symptoms. This intimate information was highly personal and very embarrassing to a reasonable person. It was not information available anywhere on the public record, as it was between Ed and the hospital staff. Ed must also argue that his accident and symptoms were not of legitimate public concern. Courier Journal will defend against this claim by stating that disclosing Ed's accident and symptoms was necessary to inform the public of the seriousness of the lack of safety precautions at local arms manufacturing facilities. However, Ed is not a public figure and the court is not likely to view the disclosure of his name and some of the highly specific descriptions of ailments as necessary to inform the public of dangerous conditions in arms manufacturing facilities. Ed will probably recover for the humiliation arising from the public disclosure.

Ed may also claim intentional misrepresentation for Ralph's action of appearing in his hospital room in attire that implied he was a doctor. In order to establish misrepresentation, Ed must prove that Ralph committed a misrepresentation, that he had a culpable state of mind, that he intended to induce Ed's reliance and that Ed suffered damages while justifiably relying on Ralph's misrepresentation. Ed possessed information that Ralph was very interested in for his newspaper story. A reporter who enters a hospital room of a sick and mentally impaired man wearing a white coat and stethoscope seeking information is likely to be found to have misrepresented himself. Courier Journal may argue that Ralph never said he was a doctor and merely failed to disclose this fact to Ed. However, it would be very difficult for Ralph to explain his attire, which is the basis for Ed's claim. The court would likely find that Ed was justified in disclosing his symptoms to Ralph because a reasonable person would have believed the reporter was a doctor.

Finally, Ed may claim intentional infliction of emotional distress. This tort occurs when the defendant intentionally or recklessly causes severe emotional damage to the plaintiff through extreme and outrageous conduct. The plaintiff must show the defendant intended to inflict distress, knew with substantial certainty that such distress would result or acted with reckless disregard of a high probability that it would occur. Ed may have difficulty proving the requisite intent or recklessness and that Ralph's conduct was extreme and outrageous.

QUESTION 21

Transco operated buses within the city. One morning, J.J., a Transco driver, awoke with a bad cold. He consulted the yellow pages of the telephone directory and called Dr. Irwin, a physician listed under the category, "Physicians — Eye, Ear, Nose & Throat." She had just started practicing as a physician two months earlier. J.J. told Dr. Irwin that he had a bad cold and was scheduled to go to work at noon that day. Dr. Irwin listened to J.J. describe his symptoms, said she could not give J.J. an appointment, and told him to buy a bottle of Pyrib at a drugstore and to use its contents as directed on the label. Pyrib was a cold remedy antihistamine prepared and marketed by Drugsco. J.J. obtained the Pyrib from a drugstore, took the first dosage called for on the label and went to work at noon.

At 2:37 p.m. that day, J.J. felt drowsy while driving his bus. However, he continued driving and shortly thereafter, fell asleep. The bus jumped a curb and hit a construction sign. Chris, a paying passenger on the bus, was injured. J.J. also suffered injuries and had his driver's license suspended for one year. The only job he could get was as a clown at children's parties for two-thirds the compensation that he received as a bus driver. He refused such employment.

Pyrib was known to cause drowsiness and sleep in about 20% of the persons who took it. Dr. Irwin did not warn J.J. that the medication she prescribed might cause drowsiness, nor did the label on the bottle contain any such warning. Both Dr. Irwin and Drugsco knew of Pyrib's side-effects.

1. What are J.J.'s rights, if any, against:

   A. Dr. Irwin? Discuss.

   B. Drugsco? Discuss.

2. What are Chris' rights, if any, against Transco? Discuss.

ISSUE/FACT LADDER

Issue	Facts
Paragraph 1 Vicarious Liability	J.J. was a bus driver with Transco, a company which operated buses within the city.
Paragraph 1 Professional Novice	Dr. Irwin had just started practicing as a physician two months earlier.
Paragraph 1 Negligence	J.J. told Dr. Irwin that he was scheduled to go to work at noon that day. Dr. Irwin listened to J.J. describe his symptoms, said she could not give J.J. an appointment, and told him to buy a bottle of Pyrib at a drug store.
Paragraph 2 Negligence / Contributory Negligence	J.J. felt drowsy while driving his bus. However, he continued driving and shortly thereafter, fell asleep. The bus jumped a curb and hit a construction sign.
Paragraph 2 Damages	Chris, a paying passenger on the bus, was injured. J.J. also suffered injuries and had his driver's license suspended for one year.
Paragraph 2 Duty to Mitigate Damages	The only job he could get was as a clown at children's parties for two-thirds the compensation that he received as a bus driver. He refused such employment.
Paragraph 3 Failure to Warn	Dr. Irwin did not warn J.J. that the medication she prescribed might cause drowsiness nor did the label on the bottle contain any such warning. Both Dr. Irwin and Drugsco knew of Pyrib's side-effects.

OUTLINE OF ISSUES

1. What are J.J.'s rights, if any, against:
   A. Dr. Irwin? Discuss.
   B. Drugsco? Discuss.
2. What are Chris' rights, if any, against Transco? Discuss.

I. J.J. v. Dr. Irwin

   Negligence

   A. Duty

   B. Breach

   C. Causation

   D. Damages

II. J.J. v. Drugsco

   Products Liability Theories

   A. Warranty

   B. Failure to Warn

III.   Chris v. Transco

   A. Vicarious Liability

   B. Negligence

      1. Duty

      2. Breach

      3. Causation

      4. Damages

SUBSTANTIVE ANSWER

I. J.J. v. Dr. Irwin

J.J. could sue Dr. Irwin for negligence. To prevail in such an action, J.J. would have to prove that Dr. Irwin owed him a duty of care and that Dr. Irwin breached that duty, causing him damages.

Dr. Irwin owed J.J. a duty to exercise reasonable care when giving him medical advice and prescribing drugs. J.J. could claim that Dr. Irwin breached that duty when she prescribed Pyrib for him without ever examining him, and without any knowledge of his medical history. He could argue that a reasonable doctor would not have prescribed a drug for a person whose medical history was not known because of the possibility of dangerous side-effects. J.J. could also claim that Dr. Irwin breached her duty when she failed to warn him that Pyrib was known to cause drowsiness and sleep in about 20% of those who take it. He could argue that by failing to inform him of this possibility, or of the fact that it might be dangerous to drive while on this medication, Dr. Irwin acted in a manner in which a reasonably careful doctor would not have acted.

Since the medical profession provides national certification, Dr. Irwin would be held to the national standard of care, not an individualized or regional standard, when determining whether her conduct breached her duty to exercise reasonable care. Furthermore, Dr. Irwin would not have a lower standard of care because she only started practicing medicine two months before. Newly licensed doctors are held to the same standard as experienced members of the profession.

"But for" Dr. Irwin's negligence in failing to warn J.J. that Pyrib might cause drowsiness and sleep, the accident would not have occurred. Dr. Irwin may argue that she was not the proximate cause of J.J.'s injuries since Drugsco was required to include a warning on its label, but failed to do so. Thus, Drugsco's negligence was a superseding cause that relieves her of liability. However, it is unlikely that this argument will be successful. It was reasonably foreseeable that not every drug on the market would have adequate warnings about its side-effects. She knew about these side-effects and should have informed her patient of their existence. She was the proximate cause of J.J.'s injuries.

Dr. Irwin might also argue that J.J. was negligent when he continued to drive despite feeling drowsy. However, it is possible that he felt drowsy, but did not believe he would fall asleep. The court will decide whether a reasonable person would have continued driving under the circumstances. If the court finds that J.J.'s actions contributed to the accident and the jurisdiction recognizes the doctrine of contributory negligence, he will be barred from recovery. However, if the jurisdiction recognizes the doctrine of comparative negligence, the court will divide the liability between Dr. Irwin and J.J. based on their relative degrees of fault.

Dr. Irwin would be liable for all actual damages that J.J. can prove. This includes damages for medical expenses, lost earnings, future earnings, mental distress and pain and suffering. Although plaintiffs have a duty to mitigate damages they can reasonably avoid, it is unlikely that J.J.'s failure to take a job as a clown, was a breach of this duty. Most courts have held that plaintiffs who seek lost income damages have no duty to obtain work outside their chosen profession.

II.   J.J. v. Drugsco

J.J. could also bring an action against Drugsco under products liability based on the theories of implied warranty and strict tort liability.

J.J. could sue Drugsco for breaching its implied warranty of merchantability. All products that are packaged in labelled bottles are assumed to be fit for the ordinary purpose for which they are intended. Drugsco, as a regular manufacturer and seller of Pyrib, created an implied warranty of merchantability when it offered Pyrib for sale to drugstores. J.J. may have a problem, however, of proving that Pyrib was not fit for its intended use. While it contained some dangerous side-effects, there is no evidence that the product did not fulfill its intended purpose, i.e., as a cold remedy. J.J. would probably do better by arguing that Pyrib was an unreasonably dangerous product because there was no warning about its side-effects.

A product that is not defectively designed or manufactured may still be considered defective if warnings are required for its safe use, and the warnings are inadequate. To satisfy its duty to warn, a manufacturer must provide a warning that adequately indicates the likelihood and severity of the drug's known risks. Drugsco failed to provide any warning about Pyrib, even though it knew that Pyrib caused drowsiness and sleep in about 20% of the persons who took it. Therefore, Pyrib is a defective product and Drugsco is strictly liable for all injuries sustained by J.J.

Drugsco may attempt to argue that it only has a duty to warn physicians of the risks of its drug, not patients. However, this exception to a manufacturer's duty to warn is only available for prescription drugs. The rationale is that the physician is in the best position to prescribe a drug and warn of its dangers. Pyrib, on the other hand, is an over the counter drug that is available to the general public. It can be obtained without a prescription, and, thus, does not fall under the exception. Drugsco will be strictly liable for failing to warn its consumers of the risks of Pyrib.

III. Chris v. Transco

An employer is liable for the torts an employee commits while acting within the scope of employment, i.e., all actions that are closely connected to the employee's work which are done to advance the employer's business interests. At the time of J.J.'s alleged negligence, he was driving a Transco bus. This was clearly within the scope of his employment as a bus driver. Therefore, Transco will be liable for all injuries that resulted from his negligence during this period of time.

Chris could argue that it was J.J.'s negligent driving which led to his injuries. As a driver of a motor vehicle, J.J. has a duty to exercise reasonable care when driving. While he has driving his bus, J.J. felt drowsy. Instead of pulling his bus off the road until he felt better, J.J. continued driving and eventually fell asleep behind the wheel. If the court determines that a reasonable driver would have pulled off the road upon feeling drowsy, J.J. will have breached his duty to exercise reasonable care.

Chris would also have to prove that J.J.'s breach of his duty was the cause of Chris' injuries. "But for" J.J.'s failure to pull off the road, the accident would not have happened. Therefore, J.J. was the actual cause of Chris' injuries. He was also the proximate cause of Chris' injuries since it is foreseeable that a person who feels drowsy may subsequently fall asleep and it is foreseeable that a person who falls asleep while driving may cause injuries to others, including any passengers within that person's vehicle.

Transco would be liable for all actual damages that Chris can prove. This includes damages for medical expenses, lost earnings, future earnings, mental distress and pain and suffering.

Transco, as a common carrier, has a greater duty of care than the average person. However, since it is unlikely that they would have known that J.J. was taking Pyrib, and it is doubtful that they should have known this, an action for negligence against Transco would probably be unsuccessful. The better strategy for Chris is to hold Transco vicariously liable for their employee's negligence.

QUESTION 22

Star stored furniture in a warehouse owned by Ware and prepaid one month's storage fees. At the end of the month, Star demanded the return of his furniture. Ware refused to surrender the furniture, claiming in good faith but mistakenly that storage fees were due. Ware informed Star that he would check to determine if the fees had been paid and would call Star if he determined payment had been made. Star heard nothing further from Ware.

The day following Star's demand, Ware contracted with Exco, a licensed exterminator, to free the warehouse of rats. Ware and Exco agreed that a poisonous gas would be used for this purpose, but all decisions about the work were left to Exco.

Two days later, before Exco had completed the job, some of the gas escaped from the warehouse into the adjoining building. Otis, an occupant of that building, was injured by inhalation of the gas. There is no evidence as to how the gas escaped into the adjoining building. All usual precautions had been taken to seal all exits and openings in the warehouse.

Gas fumes exploded when they came into contact with an open flame in the warehouse. The explosion destroyed Star's furniture. This is the first instance in which the gas used by Exco has exploded. The accepted opinion of the experts was that it was not flammable or explosive.

1. What are Star's rights, if any, against:

    A. Exco? Discuss.

    B. Ware? Discuss.

2. What are Otis' rights, if any, against:

    A. Ware? Discuss.

    B. Exco? Discuss.

ISSUE/FACT LADDER

Issue	Facts
Paragraph 1 Conversion	Star stored furniture in a warehouse owned by Ware. Star demanded the return of his furniture but Ware refused, believing in good faith that Star owed storage fees.
Paragraph 2 Independent Contractor / Vicarious Liability	Ware contracted with Exco, a licensed exterminator, to free the warehouse of rats. Both parties agreed that poison gas would be used, but all other decisions concerning the work were left to Exco.
Paragraph 2 Ultrahazardous Activity	Ware and Exco agreed that poisonous gas should be used to rid the warehouse of rats.
Paragraph 3 Private Nuisance / Damages	Some of the poisonous gas escaped to an adjoining building causing injury to Otis, an occupant of the adjoining building. There was no evidence of negligence.
Paragraph 4 Negligence / Damages	The gas used by Expo caused an explosion when its gas fumes came into contact with an open flame in the warehouse. The explosion destroyed Star's furniture.

OUTLINE OF ISSUES

1. What are Star's rights, if any, against:
   A. Exco? Discuss.
   B. Ware? Discuss.
2. What are Otis' rights, if any, against:
   A. Ware? Discuss.
   B. Exco? Discuss.

I. Star v. Exco

   A. Ultrahazardous Activity

   B. Negligence

      1. Res Ipsa Loquitur

      2. Proximate Cause

      3. Damages

II. Star v. Ware

   A. Conversion

   B. Independent Contractor / Vicarious Liability

III.   Otis v. Ware

   Independant Contractor / Vicarious Liability

IV.   Otis v. Exco

   A. Ultrahazardous Activity

   B. Private Nuisance

   C. Negligence

      1. Duty

      2. Breach

3. Causation

4. Damages

SUBSTANTIVE ANSWER

I. Star v. Exco

Star may claim that Exco is strictly liable because using poisonous and flammable gas is an ultrahazardous activity. There is strict liability for activities that involve an inherent and substantial risk of harm. However, if the gas was an ultrahazardous activity, it is only because it was poisonous, and not for any other kind of risk of harm. This case was the first instance in which the gas used by Exco exploded, and the accepted view of experts was that it was not flammable or explosive. The explosion was an unexpected phenomena for which Exco will probably not be held strictly liable.

Star should claim that Exco was negligent under the doctrine of res ipsa loquitur. This latin phrase translates roughly into "the thing speaks for itself," and is used to create an inference or presumption of negligence against the defendant by the mere fact that the accident occurred. Res ipsa loquitur applies here because a gas explosion seldom occurs without negligence, the gas was in the exclusive control of Exco and Star did not contribute to the accident. Star does not have to prove that such an accident never occurs except through someone's negligence; he must merely show that, more often than not, the defendant's negligence is the cause.

Even with the doctrine of res ipsa loquitur, Star still must prove that the accident was the proximate cause of the destruction of his property. Exco will argue that Star was not a foreseeable plaintiff nor was the destruction of his property a foreseeable harm from using poisonous gas. However, the court would probably consider Star a foreseeable plaintiff since he is part of the foreseeable class of users of Ware's warehouse. Exco probably will be liable for the explosion because an injury which is even remotely likely is considered foreseeable for purposes of liability. While the gas exploding was improbable, there was a remote possibility that it would happen and that this would cause the destruction of property. Star will recover for his property damages.

Finally, the open flame in the warehouse which came into contact with the gas fumes will not be a superseding intervening cause. Only extraordinary negligence is unforeseeable and may relieve a defendant of liability. An open flame in a warehouse could possibly be negligent but is not likely to be extraordinarily so. The open flame could have been something as insignificant as the lighting of a cigarette.

II. Star v. Ware

Star will claim that Ware is vicariously liable under the doctrine of respondeat superior for any torts committed by Exco. Under this doctrine, an employer is liable for the torts that employees commit while acting within the scope of their employment. To be classified as an employee, one must be subject to the control of the employer. However, independent contractors are not subject to the control of their employer because they more or less decide for themselves how to do the work. Exco probably qualifies as an independent contractor because all decision about the work, other than the agreement to use poison gas, were left to it.

Star may have an argument that the express agreement to use poisonous gas between Ware and Exco makes Ware vicariously liable because Ware did have control over Exco regarding this decision. In addition, Ware may have a nondelegable duty of care to the users of his warehouse which will make him liable for Exco's inadequate performance. This is a public policy decision.

Star should also bring an action against Ware under the theory of conversion. This tort occurs when the defendant so substantially interferes with the plaintiff's ownership or possession of property that the plaintiff is entitled to recover for the property's full value. The court will look at the extent and duration of the defendant's exercise of control over the property, the defendant's good faith, the harm done to the property and the inconvenience and expense caused to the plaintiff. The exact method for balancing and weighing these factors is quite imprecise. However, Ware's refusal to return the goods, even for a few days, was probably a conversion because the subsequent explosion destroyed the furniture. The court will view this as substantial interference with Star's property rights. While Ware acted in good faith in retaining the property, good faith is not necessary to establish intent. Ware only needed to have the intent to possess the property.

III.   Otis v. Ware

Otis will claim that Ware is vicariously liable under the doctrine of respondeat superior. The respondeat superior analysis used above for Star's claim against Ware also applies to Otis's claim. Again, the court would probably view Exco as an independent contractor. However, Otis's ultrahazardous activity claim is different because he was injured by the gas from inhaling its poisonous fumes. This is the kind of harm which would make the gas an ultrahazardous activity. The independent contractor exception to vicarious liability does not apply to ultrahazardous activity claims. This means that Ware may be liable to Otis for the torts committed against him by Exco.

IV.   Otis v. Exco

Otis may claim that using poisonous gas to kill rats is an ultrahazardous activity for which Exco is strictly liable. Otis is a foreseeable plaintiff who suffered injury from the foreseeable risk of exposure. It can be concluded that Exco knew of this risk to individuals like Otis because it took precautions to seal the building to insure no gas escaped. Other factors the court will consider include the degree of risk, the seriousness of the harm, whether the risk can be eliminated with due care, whether it is a common activity, the appropriateness of the activity and its value. The court may not find this activity to be ultrahazardous because a key requirement is that the activity cannot be carried out safely, even with reasonable care. It might be possible that the gassing of the warehouse could be carried out safely if better precautions are taken, suggesting a negligence claim. The court also might question the value to the community of killing rats with gas when it's possible to use alternative means like rat traps and poisonous food.

Otis might have a better chance of success with a negligence claim. Otis can argue that Exco breached its duty to exterminate rats in a manner reasonably safe to neighboring people. Exco breached either by not insuring that the gas would not escape from the building or by using poisonous gas in the first place when other methods may have been available. The release of the gas was the proximate cause of Otis' injury and he would be able to recover for all injuries sustained.

Otis may also bring a claim against Exco under trespass or nuisance. However, Otis may not be able to pursue his trespass claim because Exco did not have the intent to trespass. Exco did not intend for the gas to escape the confines of Ware's building.

Otis will have more success under a private nuisance theory. Tenants, such as Otis, may bring private nuisance suits on the grounds that they have a de facto interest in the land. Nuisance protects one's use and enjoyment of one's property from unreasonable interference. In determining unreasonableness, a court will balance the harm to the plaintiff against the benefits of the defendant's conduct to the community. As mentioned above under the ultrahazardous activity claim, the court may find the harm to Otis far outweighs the benefits to the community of using gas especially when poisonous food or traps will also kill the rats. Otis will recover for the harm suffered as a result of the nuisance. He should get pain and suffering, medical expenses and any lost earnings.

QUESTION 23

Mack suffered from severe emotional instability and was under treatment by Susan, a psychiatrist. During the course of his consultations with Susan, Mack admitted that while driving his car on the highway he would frequently experience aggressive impulses, during which he would drive directly toward another vehicle in order to frighten the driver, and, at the last moment, would swerve back into his own lane. Susan frequently counselled Mack against driving until his emotional condition improved, but Mack admitted to Susan that he was ignoring the advice.

One day, while driving on a crowded city street, Mack had one of his impulses and drove directly toward Al, another motorist, who was approaching from the opposite direction. Al, badly frightened, swerved sharply to his right in order to avoid a collision. Al did so despite his awareness that such a swerve would probably cause his car to strike Bud, who was standing on the sidewalk. Al's car struck and injured Bud. Al did not sustain any physical injury.

These events were witnessed from an upstairs window by Carrie, an elderly woman who lived nearby. Carrie sustained a disabling heart attack as a result.

I. What rights, if any, does Bud have against:

    A. Al? Discuss.

    B. Mack? Discuss.

II. What rights, if any, does Al have against:

    A. Mack? Discuss.

    B. Susan? Discuss.

III.   What rights, if any, does Carrie have against Mack? Discuss.

ISSUE/FACT LADDER

Issue	Facts
Paragraph 1 Negligence	Susan frequently counselled Mack against driving because he very often experienced aggressive impulses. Mack admitted to Susan that he was ignoring her advice.
Paragraph 2 Assault / Intentional Infliction of Emotional Distress	Mack, driven by one of his impulses, drove his car directly toward Al's car with the purpose of frightening Al.
Paragraph 2 Damages	Al was badly frightened, but did not sustain any physical injuries.
Paragraph 2 Battery / Negligence	Al swerved his car despite his awareness that this would probably cause his car to strike Bud, who was standing on the sidewalk.
Paragraph 2 Damages	Al's car struck and injured Bud.
Paragraph 3 Negligent Infliction of Emotional Distress	Carrie, an elderly woman who lived nearby, witnessed the events from an upstairs window and sustained a heart attack as a result.

OUTLINE OF ISSUES

I. What rights, if any, does Bud have against:
A. Al? Discuss.
B. Mack? Discuss.
II. What rights, if any, does Al have against:
A. Mack? Discuss.
B. Susan? Discuss.
III.   What rights, if any, does Carrie have against Mack? Discuss.

I. Bud v. Al

A. Battery

B. Negligence

II. Bud v. Mack

A. Battery

B. Negligence

III.   Al v. Mack

A. Intentional Infliction of Emotional Distress

1. Intent

2. Extreme and Outrageous Conduct

3. Severe Emotional Distress

B. Assault

IV.   Al v. Susan

Negligence / Affirmative Duty

V. Carrie v. Mack

Negligent Infliction of Emotional Distress

SUBSTANTIVE ANSWER

I. Bud v. Al

Bud will likely bring a suit against Al for the tort of battery, and argue negligence in the alternative.

To prevail in a suit for battery, Bud must prove that Al either had the specific intent to cause the contact with Bud, or that he knew with substantial certainty that the contact would result. It does not appear from the facts that Al swerved his car in order to hit Bud, but rather that he swerved to avoid being hit by Mack. Further, Al was only aware that his action would probably result in contact with Bud. Because awareness of a probability of contact would be considered short of substantial certainty, and Al did not have the specific intent to hit Bud with his car, Bud would not be able to prove that Al had the requisite intent to commit a battery.

Although Al did not have the necessary intent to commit a battery, he may still be liable for negligence. Al had a duty as a driver to avoid causing an unreasonable risk of harm to others while driving. Because Al proceeded to swerve his car despite knowledge that he would probably hit Bud, this may be considered a breach of his duty. However, Al only had a duty to act as a reasonable person under the circumstances, and a jury might find that a reasonable person faced with a life threatening emergency would have acted as Al did. Thus, whether Al is negligent will depend upon a jury's determination of what was reasonable under the circumstances.

If the jury determines that Al acted unreasonably, he will be liable for all of Bud's injuries, including medical expenses, lost present and future earnings, pain and suffering, and mental distress.

II. Bud v. Mack

Bud will probably sue Mack for battery, and argue negligence in the alternative.

As mentioned earlier, to prove battery a plaintiff must show that a defendant had the specific intent to cause contact, or knew with substantial certainty that contact would result. Mack clearly did not have the specific intent to cause contact with Bud since his actions were directed against Al. Further, transferred intent would not apply since Mack never intended to cause contact with Al; Mack intended to swerve away from Al in the last moment. Further, Mack did not know with substantial certainty that contact would result with either Al or Bud. He thought that any collision would be avoided when he swerved away. Thus, Bud would not be able to establish that Mack had the requisite intent to commit battery.

Although Mack did not commit a battery, he may have breached a duty to use reasonable care to avoid creating an unreasonable risk of harm to others. Although the actual risk was created by Mack's uncontrollable impulsive actions, and negligence liability is not generally imposed for uncontrollable conduct such as an epileptic seizure, Mack may nevertheless have breached his duty of care by driving despite Susan's recommendations that he refrain from doing so, and his knowledge that he was frequently overcome by aggressive impulses while driving. Mack's conduct will likely be deemed the proximate cause of Bud's injuries since it is foreseeable that driving directly toward another vehicle might cause that vehicle to swerve and hit another car or a bystander. Thus, Mack would likely be found liable under a negligence theory for all of Bud's injuries, including medical expenses, lost present and future earnings, pain and suffering, and mental distress.

III. Al v. Mack

Al would sue Mack for the intentional infliction of emotional distress and assault.

In order to recover for the intentional infliction of emotional distress, Al must show that Mack intended the infliction of distress, knew with substantial certainty that distress would result, or acted with reckless disregard of a high probability that distress would occur. Since Mack's purpose in driving directly toward Al was to frighten Al, it seems clear that he has satisfied the intent requirement.

To establish the intentional infliction of emotional distress, Al must also show that Mack's conduct was extreme and outrageous. Extreme and outrageous conduct is intentional conduct which exceeds all reasonable bounds of decency in a civilized society. A reasonable jury would probably find that intentionally driving head on toward another car was extreme and outrageous.

Lastly, Al would have to prove that his emotional distress was severe in order to recover for the intentional infliction of emotional distress. This would be extremely difficult since most courts will not allow recovery for emotional distress if there was no physical impact which caused the distress, or no physical manifestations of the distress. However, recovery for pure emotional distress that is unaccompanied by physical symptoms is allowed in extreme cases such as the mishandling of a corpse or the misdiagnosis of a serious illness. If the jury find this to be an extreme case, Al will be able to recover for any actual damages caused by Mack's intentional infliction of emotional distress.

Al may also try to recover from Mack for assault. Assault is defined as the intentional act of causing a reasonable apprehension of immediate harmful or offensive contact. It is likely that a jury would find that Al's apprehension was reasonable. It is unimportant that Mack had no intention of causing contact with Al, and that no contact occurred. So long as Mack intended to cause Al apprehension of imminent contact, and it appeared to Al that Mack had the present ability to cause the harmful contact, an assault may have occurred. Since Al swerved to avoid Mack, it is clear that Al perceived an imminent threat of contact, and can recover from Mack for assault.

The advantage of bringing an assault action, as opposed to an action for the intentional infliction of emotional distress, is that Al could recover without having to show actual damages — damages difficult to prove in cases of emotional distress unaccompanied by physical injury. Al would be able to recover nominal and punitive damages in an assault action.

IV. Al v. Susan

Al may try to sue Susan, Mack's psychiatrist, for negligence. For Al to prevail in a negligence suit against Susan, he must establish that Susan owed him a duty of care. Some courts have held that a doctor-patient relationship may impose an affirmative duty on the physician to warn third persons of danger posed by the patient. However, this duty to warn only extends to specifically named parties who are placed at risk by the patient, as a physician could not possibly warn all people who might be harmed by the patient. Thus, Susan had no duty to warn Al of Mack's impulsive tendencies. Al may assert that Susan had a duty to control Mack. However, many states grant doctors immunity from liability with respect to their decisions about whether to control a specific patient. Thus, it is likely that Susan did not owe Al a duty to control Mack.

V. Carrie v. Mack

Carrie may try to sue Mack for the negligent infliction of emotional distress. A few courts have allowed recovery for this tort under limited circumstances. Some courts have only allowed recovery if the plaintiff was sufficiently near the accident to have reasonably felt personally endangered by the defendant's conduct. This has been known as the "zone of danger" rule. Since Carrie was watching the accident from an upstairs window she was not within the "zone of danger." Many courts that have abandoned the "zone of danger" rule have limited recovery to foreseeable plaintiffs who are closely related to the parties involved in the accident, and who witnessed the accident from nearby. Although Carrie witnessed the accident from nearby, she was not a foreseeable plaintiff and was not a relative of either Al or Bud.

QUESTION 24

Dan, the operator of a large moving van, was approaching an intersection on a four-lane street when his engine died and the vehicle came to a complete halt in the road. He was not responsible for the engine failure or the vehicle's coming to a stop. Dan left it standing unattended while he went to secure assistance. This was a violation of a state statute making it unlawful to leave a vehicle unattended on a state highway. The van had stalled in the left lane in the direction in which it was proceeding immediately before the intersection, leaving ample room for passage in the same direction in the right lane.

After Dan had gone, Vick, driving a sports car, approached from the same direction and halted to the right of and parallel to the van in preparation of entering the intersection. The large van entirely obscured his vision to the left, but Vick decided to proceed across the intersection. As he did so, he struck a motorcycle, driven by Peter, approaching from the left on the intersecting street. Peter saw Vick's car emerging from behind the van and could have brought his cycle to a halt in time to avoid being struck had it not been for the fact that his brakes were bad. By the time that Vick had seen Peter, it was too late to stop. Peter suffered a fractured collarbone, concussion and destruction of his motorcycle in the accident. It is conceded that both Vick and Peter could have seen each other in abundant time to avoid the accident if Dan's car had not obstructed the view.

1. What are Peter's rights, if any, against Dan? Discuss.

2. What are Peter's rights, if any, against Vick? Discuss.

ISSUE / FACT LADDER

Issue	Facts
Paragraph 1 Negligence Per Se	A state statute prohibits motorists from leaving their vehicle unattended on a public highway. Dan violated the statute when he left his moving van unattended on the road after the engine had failed.
Paragraph 2 Negligence / Negligence Per Se	Vick's Volkswagen collided with Peter's motorcycle after Vick pulled out of an intersection without being able to see what was coming from his left. Vick could not see to his left because Dan's moving van obstructed his view. The accident would not have occurred had Dan's moving van not obstructed the view.
Paragraph 2 Contributory Negligence	Peter saw Vick pull out and would have been able to avoid the accident had his motorcycle not had bad brakes.

OUTLINE OF ISSUES

1. What are Peter's rights, if any, against Dan? Discuss.
2. What are Peter's rights, if any, against Vick? Discuss.

I. Peter v. Dan

    A. Negligence Per Se

        1. Causation

        2. Damages

    B. Contributory / Comparative Negligence

II. Peter v. Vick

    A. Negligence

        1. Duty

        2. Breach

        3. Causation

        4. Damages

    B. Contributory / Comparative Negligence

SUBSTANTIVE ANSWER

I. Peter v. Dan

Peter should claim that Dan is negligent per se because he violated the state statute prohibiting motorists from leaving their vehicles unattended. While courts and juries normally decide what a reasonable person would do under given circumstances, a statute effectively assumes this function. The majority of courts have held that a violation of a statute is negligent per se, but there is a minority who view such violations as only evidence of negligence that may be outweighed by other evidence showing due care.

In order for a violation of a statute to be "negligent per se," it must have a sufficiently close application to the facts. The court will make this decision by looking at the class of people the statute is intended to protect, whether the harm suffered is the type meant to be prevented and whether the standard of conduct is clearly defined in the statute.

The statute in question probably is designed to protect other motorists from the hazards created by unattended vehicles. These hazards include the accidents caused by obstructed views and the traffic jams created when confused motorists do not realize that a vehicle is unattended and will remain stationary. Motorists such as Dan are probably expected to remain with their vehicle to direct traffic around them and to generally serve as a visible warning to unsuspecting motorists that there is a problem on the road. They have a duty to mitigate the danger by alerting and assisting other motorists. The accident between Peter and Vick was the type of harm meant to be prevented by the statute.

Dan may argue that he is excused from his statutory duty because compliance was impossible. He needed assistance but could not get help and remain with his vehicle at the same time. However, the court would probably hold that compliance was possible because he could have asked another motorist to call for assistance. Dan may also argue that he was faced with an emergency he did not create since he was not responsible for the failed engine in his vehicle. The court will not be persuaded because an emergency requires that compliance with the statute involve a risk of greater harm than violation of the statute. It is unlikely that Dan would have faced a risk of harm greater than the accident if he had complied with the statute.

While the facts indicate that Dan was negligent per se, and thus no duty or breach of duty must be proved, Peter still must show there is a causal link between Dan's violation and the resulting injury. Since both Peter and Vick would have seen each other with abundant time to avoid the accident had Dan's vehicle not obstructed Vick's view, the court is likely to hold that Dan's violation was a causal link to Peter's injuries. Peter will recover for the harm suffered, including personal injuries and the damage to his motorcycle.

Dan may claim that Vick was negligent in pulling out into the intersection when he could not see around Dan's van, and that this broke the causal link between Dan's violation of the statute and the accident. However, it was reasonably foreseeable to Dan that a motorist would pull out into the intersection without being able to see what was coming from the left. Dan is liable for foreseeable negligence by motorists who could not see around his van.

Dan should claim that Peter was contributorily negligent. Peter violated his duty to reasonably protect his own safety and that of other motorists by operating his motorcycle with bad brakes. He knew or should have known they were in this condition. Peter's breach of this duty proximately contributed to his injuries because he could not stop his motorcycle to avoid the accident. If he is found contributorily negligent, it would completely bar him from any recovery.

Instead of contributory negligence, the court may apply the comparative negligence doctrine which divides liability between the plaintiff and defendant in proportion to their relative degrees of fault. Under the "pure" comparative negligence approach, Peter's recovery would be reduced by a proportion equal to the ratio between his own negligence and the total negligence contributing to the accident.

II. Peter v. Vick

Peter should bring a negligence claim against Vick because all motorists have a duty to drive safely. Vick breached this duty by pulling out into an intersection without being able to see if other vehicles were approaching. It is foreseeable to a reasonable person that other cars may be in the intersection, and that pulling out blindly would result in an accident. In addition, Peter might argue that it is the custom of drivers to use their horns to warn other drivers that they are pulling out blindly.

Vick should claim that Peter's inadequate brakes were a superseding intervening cause of the accident. However, even if Peter's inadequate brakes were unforeseeable and grossly negligent, it still led to the same type of harm as that which was threatened by Vick's negligence. The court will thus find that Vick's action was the proximate cause of the accident. Peter is entitled to recover for his injuries and the property damage to his motorcycle.

Vick may claim that Peter was contributorily or comparatively negligent. The same analysis will apply here as used above in Dan's contributory and comparative negligence claims against Peter. Peter will be able to recover the same damages he could recover against Dan.

QUESTION 25

Susan and Bill, partners in the ownership of a small private golf course, were out playing a round of golf when they saw John pulling away in Bill's golf cart. They screamed at him to get out, but John, out for a joyride, just grinned and drove off. Bill and Susan hopped in Susan's golf cart and took off in pursuit.

John exited the golf course and drove onto Alex's property in an effort to lose his pursuers. Bill and Susan also drove onto Alex's property despite Alex's frantic waving for them to stop. They quickly managed to catch John as Susan's cart was capable of much higher speed. Without further communication, Bill purposely bumped the side of John's cart, forcing him down a steep embankment and into a ditch. John was thrown from the cart and suffered a concussion and minor lacerations. The golf cart was totalled.

After calling the authorities, Susan and Bill were about to drive back to the golf course in Susan's cart when it began to rain heavily. Susan's cart was not equipped to drive safely in heavy rain as it did not have windshield wipers or all-weather tires. Instead of attempting to drive back, Susan drove her cart onto the only flat piece of ground she could find where she was sure the cart's flimsy standard emergency brake would keep it from rolling away in a heavy storm. Susan parked the cart on Alex's newly planted prize vegetable garden, entirely destroying next year's crop.

1. What are Alex's rights, if any, against:

   A. Bill? Discuss.

   B. Susan? Discuss.

2. What are Bill's rights, if any, against John? Discuss.

3. What are John's rights, if any, against Bill? Discuss.

ISSUE / FACT LADDER

Issue	Facts
Paragraph 1 Trespass	John entered Bill and Susan's privately owned golf course.
Paragraph 1 Trespass to Chattels / Recovery of Property	John stole Bill's golf cart. After yelling out for him to stop, Bill and Susan climbed into Susan's cart and pursued him.
Paragraph 2 Trespass / Recovery of Property	Bill and Susan entered Alex's property while pursuing John. Alex verbally requested that they not enter his property.
Paragraph 2 Battery / Recovery of Property	Without any further request for John to stop, Bill pulled even with the other cart and forced John down a steep embankment and into a ditch. John suffered a broken collar bone and a concussion.
Paragraph 2 Conversion	Bill's golf cart was totalled when it was forced down the embankment into the ditch.
Paragraph 3 Trespass / Necessity	Susan and Bill were about to leave Alex's property when it began to rain heavily. Susan's cart was not equipped for safe driving in the rain and she decided to leave it on Alex's property. She parked the cart on the only flat piece of ground on the property because she was concerned the flimsy emergency brake would not keep the cart from rolling away in the heavy rain. She parked on Alex's prize vegetable garden, destroying next year's crop.

OUTLINE OF ISSUES

1. What are Alex's rights, if any, against:
   A. Bill? Discuss.
   B. Susan? Discuss.
2. What are Bill's rights, if any, against John? Discuss.
3. What are John's rights, if any, against Bill? Discuss.

I. Alex v. Bill

   A. Trespass

   B. Recovery of Property

II. Alex v. Susan

   A. Trespass

   B. Trespass to Chattels

   C. Conversion

   D. Necessity

III.   John v. Bill

   A. Battery

   B. Recovery of Property

IV.   Bill v. John

   A. Trespass

   B. Trespass to Chattels

   C. Conversion

SUBSTANTIVE ANSWER

I. Alex v. Bill

Alex may claim that Bill trespassed on his property when he was pursuing John. However, Bill will claim that he had a privilege to enter Alex's land because it was not his fault that John had driven the stolen golf cart onto Alex's property. He was entitled to enter in a reasonable and peaceful manner to recapture his property even if Alex refused to allow his entry. Alex can argue that it was not reasonable and peaceful for Bill to pursue John in a golf cart, given that it was a dangerous and destructive chase. If the court decides Bill's actions were not reasonable, there is no privilege, and he is liable for his trespass.

II. Alex v. Susan

Alex will also bring a claim against Susan under either trespass to chattel or conversion for Susan's act of destroying his vegetable garden. A trespass to chattel is the intentional interference with property that belongs to someone else. Susan intended to park on the vegetable garden and this resulted in injury to Alex. Alex is entitled to his actual damages.

The court might view Susan's tort as a conversion since her action of parking the cart ruined the next year's crop. It is often difficult to draw the line between what is merely a trespass to chattel and what constitutes a conversion. The court will look at the extent and duration of Susan's control over the property, Susan's good faith, the harm and the inconvenience and expense caused to Alex. The court is likely to hold this was a conversion because the crop was destroyed. Although Susan may have been acting in good faith in parking on the garden, she still had the intent to park there. The court would probably regard this as dispositive.

Susan should argue that she had a privilege to park on the garden under the doctrine of necessity because she acted to protect life and property. However, a private necessity gives a defendant only a limited privilege. At most, Susan may have had the right to park the cart but she still would have to pay for all the damages she caused to Alex's property. This limited privilege means that Susan is still liable for any actual damage, but she is not liable for nominal damages even though she had technically committed a trespass.

Susan will not be successful arguing that she acted to protect life. While it may have been dangerous to drive back to the golf course in the rain, the act she is being held responsible for is her choice of parking spaces. She could have refrained from parking in the vegetable garden. It is probably too tenuous an argument to claim that parking the cart anywhere else might have resulted in danger to someone, although it could have rolled off and possibly struck and injured someone.

Susan might have a better argument that she was justified in acting to protect property. A party is privileged to interfere with another's property to avoid an injury threatened by some force of nature or from some independent cause not connected to the property owner. The court must weigh the harm to Alex's property against the likelihood and severity of the danger Susan sought to avoid. In any case, as mentioned above, Susan must still pay for the damages.

III.   Bill v. John

Bill has a claim against John for trespass on the golf course. A trespass to land is the intentional invasion of another's interest in the exclusive possession of his land. This course was privately owned by Bill and Susan and it is highly doubtful that they had consented to John's presence. John intended to enter the land and Bill may recover for nominal as well as actual damages that may have directly and proximately resulted from the trespass.

Bill also has a claim against John for trespass to chattels or conversion for John's stealing of the golf cart. A trespass to chattel is the intentional interference with property that belongs to someone else. John intended to take possession of the golf cart, and Bill will recover for actual damages.

Given the severity of the damage to the cart, Bill may recover under the doctrine of conversion instead of trespass to chattel. A conversion is the interference with another's property that is so substantial that the original possessor loses title to the property and is entitled to full compensation. Theft is one of the categories that qualifies as a conversion. While John may not have intended for the cart to be destroyed, his intent to steal the cart makes him liable.

IV.   John v. Bill

John may have a cause of action for battery. This tort is defined as the causing of harmful or offensive contact to a plaintiff's person with intent to make contact. It is not necessary that Bill make physical contact with John, the indirect contact of bumping John's cart is sufficient. While Bill may not have intended to harm John, he did intend to make the contact. If this is a battery, Bill would be liable for all consequences which ensued from his act regardless of whether they were foreseeable. John would be entitled to recover for his physical injuries.

Bill will argue that he has a privilege to recover his property. Property owners have this privilege when they use reasonable and nondeadly force while in hot pursuit of the actual wrongdoer who had taken the property, and the wrongdoer has not responded to the property owner's demand to return the property. Bill yelled at John to stop as he was stealing the cart and John's injuries occurred during the ensuing pursuit. Whether it was reasonable for Bill to force John down the embankment will be a factual question for the jury. Such force would seem capable and even likely of causing serious and even deadly harm.

Guaranteed Pass Program for the California Bar

The bottom line at *DeSario & Associates* is: WE DO NOT TEACH YOU THE LAW, WE TEACH YOU TO WRITE THE LAW. We offer something the competition can't provide. Innovative programs for a difficult exam are our specialty. If you cannot afford to fail, you should give us a call. You deserve the chance, and we want the opportunity to help you...

DeSario & Associates, led by Daniel DeSario:

- Former Director for all major California Bar Reviews
- Co-author Blond's Essay Exam Series
- Special programs for out-of-state and foreign attorneys
- One-on-one tutorial programs is our specialty
- Small group tutorial programs available. Limited to eight students.
- Over a decade of successful experience preparing thousands of students from all the major Bar Review courses.

- FREE Grade Card Analysis
- FREE Initial consultation
- One-on-one performance approaches
- Unlimited writing
- Study group discounts

- Specialized essay workshops
- Multistate tutorials
- Day-to-day study plans
- The best performance exam approach available

- Locations throughout Southern California

LIMITED ENROLLMENT

DeSario & Associates

Legal Education Consultants
4520 Van Nuys Blvd., Suite 770
Sherman Oaks, CA 91403

Southern California (Los Angeles)
(818) 783-5550 FAX (818) 783-0015

Southern California (Orange County)
(714) 565-3199

CALIFORNIA'S LEADER IN INDIVIDUAL TUTORING

DESARIO & ASSOCIATES IS NOT AFFILIATED WITH SULZBURGER & GRAHAM PUBLISHING LTD.

BLOND'S™ LAW GUIDES

Precisely What You Need to Know

- **Hanau Charts** — Flow charts for organization
- **Case Clips** — Facts, issue, and rule for every case
- **Outlines** — Concise arrangement of the law
- **Mnemonics** — Memory aids and tricks

$13.99 per copy, keyed to the following texts:

Property Dukeminier Ed.

Property General Edition
Browder
Casner
Cribbet

Torts Prosser Edition

Torts General Edition
Epstein
Keeton
Franklin

Constitutional Law
Barrett
Brest
Ducat
Gunther
Lockhart
Rotunda
Stone

Criminal Law
Kadish
LaFave
Kaplan
Weinreb
Dix
Johnson
Inbau

Corporate Tax
Lind
Kahn
Wolfman
Surrey

Corporations
Cary
Choper
Hamilton
Henn
Jennings
Solomon
Vagts

Family Law
Areen
Foote
Krause
Wadlington

Administrative Law
Bonfield
Breyer
Gellhorn
Cass
Schwartz
Mashaw

International Law
Sweeney
Henkin

Income Tax
Klein
Andrews
Surrey
Kragen
Freeland
Graetz

Civil Procedure
Cound
Field
Rosenberg
Louisell

Contracts Farnsworth Edition

Contracts General Edition
Dawson
Kessler
Fuller
Murphy
Calamari

Criminal Procedure
Kamisar
Saltzburg
Weinreb/Crim.Process
Weinreb/Crim.Justice
Miller

Evidence
McCormick
Green
Weinstein
Kaplan
Cleary

ORDER TODAY, Books Shipped Within 24 Hours!
800•366•7086

BLOND'S™ LAW GUIDES

SoftwareEdition

The electronic versions of Blond's Law Guides contain the COMPLETE Hanau Charts, Case Clips, Outlines and mnemonics you love! The programs contain many innovative features including:

- **Links** — You can instantaneously jump between Hanau Charts, cases, outlines, and related mnemonics.
- **Reader's Notes** — You can add your own notes. The program shows you which notes are yours and which are Blond's.
- **Searches** — You can perform complex Boolean Searches. No more wasting time turning pages!
- **History function** — Records your study time and progress.
- **Bookmark** — Allows automatic return to the last screen studied when restarting the program.
- **Simple to use** — No computer experience required!

IBM compatible, requires EGA or VGA graphics, mouse recommended, 3.5", 5.25" disks available.

$27.99 per copy, keyed to the following texts:

Property	Constitutional Law	Criminal Law	Civil Procedure
Dukeminier	Barrett	Kadish	Cound
Browder	Brest	LaFave	Field
Casner	Ducat	Kaplan	Rosenberg
Cribbet	Gunther	Weinreb	Louisell
	Lockhart	Dix	
Torts	Rotunda	Johnson	**Contracts**
Prosser	Stone	Inbau	Farnsworth
Epstein			Dawson
Keeton			Kessler
Franklin			Fuller
			Murphy
			Calamari

ORDER NOW! 800•366•7086

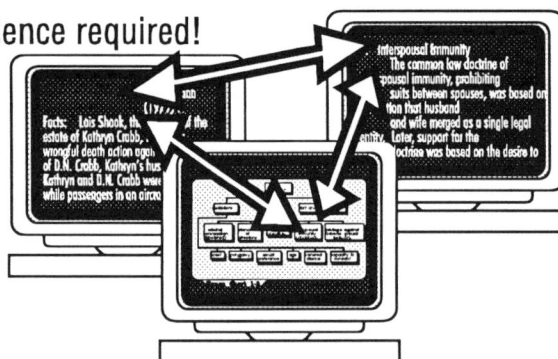

BLOND'S™
PRACTICE QUESTIONS

Multiple Choice Questions
• Practice questions arranged by subject • Answers • Explanations

Multistate Questions   **$29.99**
  Covers: Torts, Property, Contracts, Criminal Procedure,
       Criminal Law, Evidence
Professional Responsibility Questions   **$19.99**

New! Software Edition
•Multiple Choice Questions on Computer
• Complete questions, answers, and explanations from books
• Your responses scored and timed • Testing and study modes

Multistate Questions — Software   **$49.99**
Professional Responsibility — Software   **$33.99**

BLOND'S™ ESSAY SERIES
Half your grade is your ability to organize an essay;
Blond's shows and teaches you how!
• Complex essay questions • Outline of facts and issues
• Complete model answers

Essay Questions — Contracts   **$19.99**
Essay Questions — Torts   **$19.99**
Essay Questions — Criminal Law   **$19.99**

ORDER FORM

Order today! All orders shipped within 24 hours of receipt.
Mail To:
SULZBURGER & GRAHAM PUBLISHING Ltd.
PO Box 20058
Park West Station, New York NY 10025
(800) 366-7086 (212) 769-9738 FAX orders: (212) 769-9675

Please send me BLOND'S ...

Name of product	Software or Book?	Casebook You Use	Price

Shipping & Handling ___ $2.25

Total _____

Name _____

Address _____

City/State/Zip _____

Graduation _____

Day Phone _____

I Prefer:
○ 5¼ inch diskettes
○ 3½ inch diskettes

○ Check or money order enclosed (payable to Sulzburger & Graham Publishing)
○ MasterCard ○ Visa ○ American Express ○ Optima ○ DiscoverCard

_____ _____ _____
Charge Card Number   **Expiration**   **Signature**

All orders are shipped UPS same or next business day. Delivery time will vary, based on distance from New York City. Washington/Boston corridor can expect delivery 2 working days after shipment. West Coast should allow 6 working days. Overnight, 2nd day and COD available at extra cost. We cannot deliver to PO Boxes.